BOYS WILL BE BOYS

BOYS WILL BE BOYS

INSPIRING STORIES FOR SMART KIDS

APARNA JAIN

Art Director: Ayesha Broacha

cntxt

First published by Context, an imprint of Westland Publications Private Limited, in 2019

Published by Context, an imprint of Westland Books, a division of Nasadiya Technologies Private Limited, in 2023

No. 269/2B, First Floor, 'Irai Arul', Vimalraj Street, Nethaji Nagar, Alapakkam Main Road, Maduravoyal, Chennai 600095

Westland, the Westland logo, Context and the Context logo are the trademarks of Nasadiya Technologies Private Limited, or its affiliates.

ISBN: 9789395767545

10 9 8 7 6 5 4 3

Printed at Thomson Press India Private Limited

For

Anisha Bhandary
&
Mahesh Rao

Friends close but far
who raise the friendship bar.
We pretend to think
but often just drink.

CONTENTS

PREFACE

'When will you write a book on men?' I've been asked this question over and over again by teenagers and parents in the past year. Do we need another book on men? I wondered. Aren't there tomes out there? Shouldn't I be doing another volume on women?

I thought about it some more. Women aren't the only ones subject to patriarchy. For men, the pressure to conform starts at an early age, with constant rebukes: Don't cry like a girl, stop being a sissy, don't let a girl get the better of you. These and other comments are thrown so casually at them. Not just by bullies at school, but even by parents and educators.

Yes, I decided, this was a book worth attempting.

I would write about men that children may or may not have heard of. Courageous men. Men of intellect. Men who connected with the world differently. I would provide a glimpse into their lives and leave the rest to imagination – and Google. I used a mix of parameters to choose the individuals I would write about and I discovered some incredible men. Men who worked in science, music, fashion and art. Men who built rockets and businesses. An Olympian and a Paralympian, a children's writer, an investigative journalist, a psychiatrist.

All these men were aided by their inherent male privilege, some by caste and class privileges as well. I had to funnel and sift and then sift some more. I knew I was playing gatekeeper, but tokenism was something I was determined to steer clear of.

My publisher Karthika sympathised and was my biggest cheerleader, not least because she has two sons and felt this book was needed. After several months of back and forth, and innumerable conversations with friends and on social media, we finally agreed on a list of forty-five men who we all felt made the cut.

Oxfam India came on board once again as the art patron, which made it possible for twenty-seven artists to showcase their arresting interpretations of these life stories. As with *Like a Girl*, Ayesha Broacha directed the art with a sharp eye.

There was a point, I must confess, in the wake of the #MeToo movement, when inertia set in. Friends asked, 'What if someone is accused of sexual harassment after your book is published?' It took several weeks of soul searching before I could answer, 'If someone is found culpable, so be it!' Children would hear about it, and even that would be a lesson. After all, I hadn't shied away from pointing out the bad in *Like a Girl*.

Were there hurdles along the way? Of course! Mails and calls went unanswered. Tantrums were thrown. Excuses were made. Some men even ghosted me! I had to drop some of the stories I had written and art I had commissioned. But I refused to give up.

And now, a full twelve months later, here we are. In a world that is bereft of positive role models, I offer you the companion volume to *Like a Girl*. I urge you to read the short biographies, then go explore and learn more about the people here. Share the stories with your friends and families.

'Boys will be boys' has long been used as a feeble excuse for bad behaviour. I hope the stories in this book will inspire you to turn this phrase on its head.

APARNA JAIN
October 2019

BOYS
WILL BE
BOYS

Illustrated by Priya Khatri

J.R.D. TATA

THE MAN WHO BUILT TOMORROW

Jeh was standing on the balcony of the family home in France with a classmate. Hard straw hats were the rage in those days, and they were waiting for someone wearing one to pass. Whenever someone did, the boys would throw a pea at the hat and it would bounce off noisily. The man would jump out of his skin and look around, but the friends would duck and hide. One day, they heard someone knocking on their door. They had hit a teacher from school who had recognised them!

The legendary airman Louis Blèriot lived next door to the beach home the family owned in France, and Jeh was friends with his son Blèriot Jr. They would often help push Louis' airplane into its hangar. Jeh was fascinated with the flying machine and thought, 'One day, I will fly a plane too.'

In 1923, Jeh was sent to a 'crammer school' in England to learn English and prepare for Cambridge University. But as a citizen of France, he was summoned for a mandatory spell with the French Army. Luckily, an officer discovered Jeh could read, write and type, so instead of doing equestrian duty, he was appointed a secretary.

When he finished his stint, he was summoned again – this time by his father, to India. Jeh arrived at the Tata Office in Bombay as an unpaid intern. When he was twenty-two and in Jamshedpur, working at the steel factory there, his father passed away. Jehangir was now the head of the Tata family. He worked hard to pay off loans by selling his family home and moved into the Taj Mahal hotel with his siblings. 'I have great admiration for the legacy of my father and Jamsetji,' he thought. 'I want to be worthy of the Tatas.' He renounced his French passport and became an Indian citizen.

In 1929, a flying club opened in Bombay, and Jeh immediately enrolled for classes. Within twelve days, he got an 'A' licence. He was thrilled! 'No document has ever given me such joy as this blue and gold certificate,' he said. Soon, Jeh was off to London to buy a light Gypsy Moth. Then Jeh contacted the government which, after much dilly-dallying, gave him permission to start a flying mail service. In 1932, he climbed into a Puss Moth, branded Tata Air Lines, with a load of cargo mail from Karachi to Bombay. When he landed, the postmaster general of Bombay received him and the mail. 'The inaugural flight from Karachi to Bombay is my most cherished memory,' said Jehangir.

Jeh resisted the British Raj in India, just as Jamsetji Tata had done. Once, while driving back from their honeymoon, he and his wife were stuck in traffic. The hold-up was to let the Governor of Bengal pass. When Jeh saw the Governor's car arrive, he stepped in front of it and shouted, 'What do you British think of yourselves? Aren't you ashamed of holding back hundreds of Indians for your comfort?' Thelma yelled right along with him. They became the talk of the town in both Calcutta and Bombay.

Then tragedy struck again. When Jehangir was thirty-four, the chairman of Tata Sons passed away. Now, he found himself at the helm of things. He made swift, bold changes. He started building a vast empire – a chemical factory in Mithapur, Tata Chemicals; a brand for beauty products, Lakmè. When a young man called Homi Bhabha wrote to him about setting up an independent research company for the study of cosmic rays, the Tata Institute of Fundamental Research was established. He also founded India's first cancer hospital – Tata Memorial Trust – and started the Tata Engineering and Locomotive Company (TELCO), now Tata Motors.

Jeh rebranded Tata Air Lines as Air India and listed it as a public limited company. Air India bought the first Boeing in Asia and were soon flying passenger jets. The famous maharaja mascot was born!

But then, after the Emergency, the government nationalised the airline. Prime Minister Morarji Desai removed Jehangir as Chairman of Air India. An infuriated Jeh heard the announcement on the radio.

As he grew older, Jehangir would talk about stepping down from Tata Sons, but he was always pressurised to stay on. 'Do you want me to go on until I go gaga?' he would ask them. Finally, he passed on his mantle to Ratan Tata.

Jehangir died at the age of eighty-nine and left a lasting legacy. Despite being the scion of an empire, he was known for his simplicity and fairness. He believed in one rule: 'Strive for perfection, and you will reach excellence.'

HOMI BHABHA

A STELLAR LIFE

Homi and his brother were at their home in Bombay. They were listening to the plaintive strains of the violin coming from the gramophone player. Their mother often told Homi that, even as a baby, listening to music calmed him down.

Homi's father wanted him to study mechanical engineering so he could join the Tata Steel Company. When he turned eighteen, Homi left for Cambridge. Soon afterwards, his father received a pleading letter. 'Engineering is not for me. Physics is my line, and I am burning with desire to do physics...' His father agreed, reluctantly and on one condition: 'Get a first class in mechanical engineering, and then I will fund two years of additional study.' An elated Homi got a first class in both engineering and mathematics and went on to get a doctorate.

In 1939, Homi returned to India for a holiday, but the war in Europe prevented him from heading back. The physicist C.V. Raman convinced him to join the Indian Institute of Science (IISc) in Bangalore where he began researching cosmic physics, balloon flights and experimental science. Soon, another young scientist joined them; his name was Vikram Sarabhai. The two got along famously and would often attend concerts together after work. While Homi enjoyed Western ballet and music, young Vikram preferred to listen to M.S. Subbulakshmi and other Indian artistes.

Homi was frustrated with the state of scientific research in India, especially in the field of nuclear science. He wrote to his friend J.R.D. Tata, who guided him to the Dorabji Tata Trust. Homi's passionate letter to the director of the trust was thirteen pages long! 'There are so many amazing scientists in India, but no place for structured research. We lack the support and a venue,' he wrote. In 1945, the Tata Institute of Fundamental Research (TIFR) was founded in Bombay with funding from both the trust and the central government.

Homi invited leading scientists and mathematicians to join him, and gave them a free hand. Prime Minister Jawaharlal Nehru encouraged his vision and efforts. They were so close that Homi was one of the very few people to call Nehru 'Bhai'.

Homi also supported the work of young artists and bought over two hundred pieces of art for the centre. He even commissioned M.F. Husain to paint a large mural in the office, for the princely sum of ten thousand rupees.

Homi spent hours sketching his plans for the soon-to-be-established Atomic Energy Centre at Trombay. Sometimes he would telephone the architect after dinner. 'Are you doing anything tonight, Rustom?' That was code for 'Come over – now.'

Homi would then unveil new artwork for some part of the building. He had a fine eye for detail – from paint swatches and washbasins to gardens. He wanted Trombay to be the Versailles of the scientific community. And it was!

Once, a senior scientist received a phone call about a secret project. He was told, 'Write this down and give it to Dr Bhabha when you see him.' When the scientist got into Dr Bhabha's car, he handed him the paper. Bhabha read it and said, 'This is still a secret; destroy it.' The scientist immediately tore it up and threw the pieces out of the car. Bhabha admonished him: 'You did well in destroying that piece of paper, but you should not clutter the streets.'

In 1962, Bhabha asked Vikram Sarabhai to join the centre as the head of the Indian Space Programme. Four years later, he was flying to Vienna for a meeting when his plane crashed near Mont Blanc. He was only fifty-six years old when he died.

In 1967, the Atomic Energy Commission, which Homi had so lovingly designed, was renamed the Bhabha Atomic Research Centre.

Illustrated by Joanna Mendes

VIKRAM SARABHAI

ROCKET MAN

Even as a child, Vikram was multifaceted. He learnt the sitar, he learnt Manipuri dance. But what he loved best was to cycle at full speed, hands free. He would place his feet on the handlebars and sometimes even close his eyes. 'Open your eyes and hold the handle, Vicky!' his family would scream at him anxiously.

Like Homi Bhabha, Vikram went to Cambridge to study science. He managed to graduate before the war broke out. His father called and asked him to return home. 'I am worried about you. Please come back home to India!'

'Will I be able to continue my postgraduate research in India?' Vikram asked his professors. 'Only if you work under the supervision of C.V. Raman,' they said. So off went Vikram, to IISc. This is where he first met Homi Bhabha. He also met the dancer Mrinalini Swaminadhan. They fell in love and got married.

In 1943, when Gandhi announced the 'Quit India' movement, Vikram's father was concerned. 'It is getting even more dangerous. Come home to Ahmedabad soon!' he said. Vikram and Mrinalini went to Ahmedabad, where Vikram immersed himself in work. But he wanted to complete his doctorate, so a few years later, the couple was off again, to Cambridge. By the time they came back, India was independent.

In 1962, Vikram set up the Indian National Committee for Space Research (INCOSPAR) with the support of Homi Bhabha. Each time he visited his family in Ahmedabad, Vikram would carry new toys for the children. Sometimes he would casually walk over to them while they were playing and say, 'Would you let me see that toy?' When they handed it over, he would tinker with it, open it up, take out all the parts, examine them closely and walk away – abuzz with new ideas. His kids would be left with the dismantled toys!

As the chairman of INCOSPAR, Vikram had a formidable task – setting up India's rocket programme. He and his team spent two days flying over potential sites. Then, a few days later, the venue for the rocket project was fixed: a fishing village called Thumba.

The big day for India's first rocket launch was approaching. But there was one snag after another. First, the truck carrying the NASA-built rocket broke down, then the guided part of the rocket built by the French didn't fit. So some of the scientists, including a young Abdul Kalam, scraped the rocket by hand. Parts of the rocket were even transported using bicycles! The crane that had to place the rocket on the hydraulic launcher stopped working, so the rocket had to be shifted by human hands. Then the system to launch the rocket malfunctioned. Despite so many things going wrong, Vikram and his team remained calm and worked their way through every problem.

At 6.25 p.m., on 21 November 1963, the Nike–Apache rocket was in the air and bolting into space! Everyone jumped with excitement, even the very proper Homi Bhabha. Vikram sent home a telegram: 'Gee whiz wonderful rocket shot.'

When Bhabha passed away, Vikram inherited his vision for a nuclear India. But everyone only asked him questions about the atomic bomb. 'What about the bomb?' 'How long will it take us to make it?' 'Will we make a prototype? Vikram answered, 'A prototype is a "paper tiger"and paper tigers do not provide security. A bomb will not protect our country. What we need now is development.' Vikram firmly believed that communication and education in the rural areas were of foremost importance.

On 30 December 1971, Vikram inaugurated the Thumba railway station. Later that night, he passed away in his hotel room in Kovalam.

Vikram had once told his daughter Mallika, 'When you stand above the crowd, you must be ready to have stones thrown at you.' When his body was flown back to Ahmedabad, Mallika lit the pyre – breaking a centuries-old tradition!

SAM MANEKSHAW

INDIA'S BRAVEHEART

Sam's older brothers had been sent to England to study. Sam was keen on becoming a gynaecologist. His father, a doctor, said, 'Son, if you do well in your Senior Cambridge exams, I will send you to England.' But when Sam topped his class with distinction, his father said, 'My son, I'll keep my promise to you. But you are only fifteen years old. I'll send you when you are eighteen.' Angry at the delay, Sam didn't speak to his father for eighteen months. One day, he saw a newspaper advertisement for enlistment in the army. He borrowed five hundred rupees from his mother and went to Delhi to take the exam.

Sam joined the first batch of the Indian Military Academy (IMA) in Dehradun. The Adjutant Captain's name was J.F.S. McLaren. When Sam was commissioned, he too wanted such impressive initials. To his name, Sam added his father's, grandfather's and great-grandfather's initials, and called himself S.H.F.J. Manekshaw! His first year was with the Royal Scots, who couldn't pronounce his name, so they just called him Mister Mackintosh!

In 1942, when the British Army went to war against Burma, Captain Sam Manekshaw and his troops defended the bridge over the Sittaung river with great valour. A Japanese soldier emptied nine bullets into Sam's belly and lungs. No one thought he would survive. His English commander removed his own Military Cross and pinned it on the severely wounded Sam. Semi-conscious, he was taken to a hospital thirty-six hours after he was wounded.

Sam's orderly, Sher Singh, went looking for a doctor. He found an Australian surgeon, and told him that Sam had been shot in the stomach and lungs. Stomach and lung wounds were almost always fatal, so the doctor replied, 'Then I won't waste my time on him!' Sher Singh insisted and took the doctor to see the now-conscious Sam. 'What happened to you, young chap?' the doctor asked. Always one for jokes, Sam said, 'A bloody mule kicked me.' The doctor laughed. 'I see you have a sense of humour. You might be worth saving!' he said and wheeled Sam into surgery.

In 1947, when India became independent, two countries were born: India and Pakistan. Prime Minister Jinnah said, 'Stay in Pakistan, Sam.' But Sam came to India and joined the Gorkha Rifles as their first non-British officer. Once, he asked a Gurkha sentry, '*Tere naam ke cho*?' (What is your name?) '*Harka Bahadar Guru*!' the sentry replied. Sam mischievously said, '*Mere naam ke cho*?' (What is my name?) The sentry was taken aback and said, 'Sam Bahadar!' Sam loved the name, and it stuck for life: Sam Bahadur or Sam the Brave.

In 1962, China attacked an unprepared India. Sam was the Commandant at the Staff College in Willingdon when Nehru called him. 'I have a vigorous enemy, Sam. Will you take over this battle?' Sam salvaged the battered morale of the soldiers, and with the help of the Air Force, tried to bring the situation under control.

In 1969, when Indira Gandhi was prime minister, Sam got a phone call. 'Sam, you have been appointed Chief of the Army Staff by Mrs Gandhi.' Sam went to his wife and said, 'Darling, aren't you happy?' She turned to him and said, 'Well, I always knew you were going to be Chief.'

Sam and Mrs Gandhi shared a great rapport. In April 1971, a revolution was brewing in East Pakistan. Indira Gandhi said to him, 'Sam, look at these reports about how unhappy people are!' Sam said, 'Prime minister, what does it have to do with me?' She said, 'I want you to march into East Pakistan!' 'But that would mean war!' Sam retorted. 'If it's war, it's war!' said Mrs Gandhi. Sam said, 'Have you read the Bible, prime minister? It says, "Let there be light." And here you are saying, let there be war!' Eventually, Sam relented.

On 4 December at 4 a.m. – four was Sam's lucky number – the Indian Army attacked the Pakistani fighters in East Pakistan. Every morning, at 8.30 a.m., Sam would meet the prime minister for coffee and brief her on the war proceedings. The war lasted thirteen days, and 93,000 Pakistani soldiers surrendered. Bangladesh became an independent country, and Sam was a hero – again.

In 1973, the prime minister gave Sam the title of 'Field Marshal'. A fortnight later, he decided to retire from active service and moved to Coonoor with his wife. He had spent forty years in the Indian Army.

He died in 2008 after an illness that required hospitalisation. His last words were, 'I'm okay.'

216
SAM MANEKSHAW

Illustrated by Tanya Eden

ARUN KHETARPAL

A HEROIC LIFE

Arun's parents had gone out for dinner, and he and his younger brother Mukesh sneaked into their room. Their father was a colonel in the Army Corps. His ironed and polished uniform was laid out, ready for the next day. Arun put on his father's cap and shirt. Mukesh tried on the belt. 'Eyes right!' shouted Arun, as they marched up and down the room. When their father came back, the two were in big trouble!

Colonel Khetarpal was keen that Arun become an engineer and Mukesh join the army. When Arun finished school, he applied to both the Indian Institute of Technology (IIT) and the National Defence Academy (NDA). He cracked both entrance exams. He told his mother, 'Mamma, I want to join the army, but I can't tell daddy. You tell him, please?' For three months, Arun's father tried to convince him to join the IIT, but Arun was insistent.

In 1968, Arun entered the NDA and was soon headed to the Indian Military Academy (IMA). There, he set his sights on the 'Sword of Honour' – an award for the best cadet. Three weeks before his graduation, Arun's best friend's sister was getting married. His friend said, 'Let's sneak out during the weekend and take a shared cab from Dehradun to Delhi!' This was a serious breach of discipline. As the taxi filled up, to their dismay, a senior officer slid into the front seat. He didn't say much to them then, but when they returned, Arun was out of the running for the Sword of Honour. The loss stayed with him.

When he graduated as a gentleman cadet, Arun was assigned to the Poona Horse. At the dining-in ceremony, every officer had to raise a toast. When it was Arun's turn, he said, 'This is a toast to Lieutenant Colonel Ardheshir Tarapore, a Param Vir Chakra from the Poona Horse. Cheers!' Everyone raised their glass and drank. Arun continued, 'And this is a toast to the next Param Vir Chakra, Arun Khetarpal.' That's how keen he was on winning an award!

Arun was soon off to Ahmednagar for training at the Young Officers Corps. It was December 1971, and India was suddenly at war for the liberation of East Pakistan. The programme was suspended, and everyone was sent back. When Arun reached Delhi, his regiment was already on the move towards India's western flank, where the Pakistan Army was trying to gain territory.

Arun went home to meet his family for a few hours. His mother hugged him and said, 'Fight like a lion.' As he drove him to the railway station, his father said, 'Beta, make yourself, your regiment and the country proud!'

When Arun reached his destination, his commanding officer (CO) Colonel Hanut Singh said, 'Arun, I cannot send you to the front. You haven't completed your course.' But Arun was so insistent that Singh arranged a crash course for him. Arun familiarised himself with every aspect of the tank that he would be assigned to. His CO had no reason to refuse him now.

While Pakistan lost the war and surrendered to India in the east, things were different in the west. Three Indian regiments had established a bridgehead across the river Basantar, which the Pakistan Army was preparing to ram through. Things looked bleak, and the Poona Horse regiment was called to help.

Eventually, only three tanks were left defending the bridgehead. Captain Malhotra, commander of one of the tanks, sent a message to the CO: 'Hello Tiger, my gun is defective. Request permission to pull back and repair it.' Singh responded, 'No, we will fight it out from where we stand. No one will pull back an inch!' Meanwhile, the second tank's commander, Lieutenant Alhawat, was injured. Now, all the responsibility fell on Arun's shoulders – he was in command of the third tank. Arun identified and destroyed the lead enemy tank. He managed to destroy two more before his own tank was hit and caught fire.

Captain Malhotra immediately commanded him to abandon his tank. 'No sir, I will not abandon my tank. My gun is still working, and I will get them, ' Arun responded. Malhotra said, 'Get out of that tank or you'll get killed!' But Arun just turned off the wireless!

The twenty-one-year-old went on to destroy a total of eight enemy tanks. The Pakistanis began to retreat, but one of their guns managed to hit Arun's tank. And he died a hero. His family only got to know nine days later, after his body had been cremated.

Second Lieutenant Arun Khetarpal was posthumously awarded the nation's highest gallantry award – the Param Vir Chakra. His prophecy did come true. Just not in the way anyone could have imagined.

M.F. HUSAIN

BAREFOOT PAINTER

Maqbool was busy 'making his own movie' after having secretly watched a film. He painted a watercolour sequence on a paper roll, with frames featuring a bullock cart and a farmer. He attached the roll to opposite ends of a spooled box and rotated them manually. Ta-da! His very own hand-painted movie strip.

At school, Maqbool spent more time on art and football than on school-work. He used to accompany artist N.S. Bendre on his sketching trips. Bendre told Maqbool's father, 'Your son is extraordinarily talented!' But his father was worried. 'How will he earn a living?' Soon, Maqbool wanted to stop studying. 'I want to paint. If nothing works out, I can whitewash walls.' His father reluctantly agreed and Maqbool didn't go to college. His paintbrush became his teacher, and he painted in Indore for two years, non-stop.

When Maqbool was nineteen, his father lost his job. Maqbool decided to go to Bombay to earn some money. He met with a film-hoarding artist known to his family and said, 'Please help me, Shahab sa'ab.' The man replied, 'You can assist me, but only for a few months. Your kind of painting isn't welcome!' So, for the next three months, Maqbool primed and stretched cloth, mixed paints and learnt to build a wooden frame. He realised that he liked making large paintings and posters. All this time, he lived on the streets.

After this, Maqbool began to work with a leading poster artist, and quickly became the most sought-after billboard artist in Bombay. He would paint outdoors in studios compounds, which sometimes did not have electricity. Maqbool thought, 'I can only paint by day. Why am I wasting time enlarging my posters from photos so tediously with the help of a graph paper? Let me work freehand to save time.' He taught himself how to bring scale, foreshortening and perspective to massive posters.

Illustrated by Sanchita Jain

When India gained independence, Maqbool – now known as M.F. Husain – founded the Progressive Artists' Group along with five other artists. Each had a unique style but a common purpose – to focus on Indian art and Indian subjects.

In 1954, Husain met Qi Baishi, a ninety-year-old Chinese master artist. His canvas of a thousand horses was haunting. Husain used to paint the Dudul horses as a child and now he started again. Horses became his signature motif. He painted horses from Indian history and mythology – from Ashwamedha to Chetak.

In 1968, Husain read A. Rajagopalachari's *Ramayana* and *Mahabharata* and began painting his own versions of the epics. When Puri Shankaracharya came to see his work, he exclaimed, 'Your *sanskars* must be Hindu, Husain. You could not have made such incredible paintings otherwise!' Curious, some well-known Muslims came to see his paintings. 'How come you aren't painting Islamic history, Husain?' they asked. He replied, 'Do you have the tolerance that Hindus have?'

Once, Husain met Mother Teresa. He thought, 'I have to paint her as the destitute and the dying see her. I must capture the hope she gives them.' He made a series of paintings which would show at the opening of a new ITDC hotel in Cyprus. The afternoon before the opening, the chairman of the hotel went to meet Husain. 'Husain sa'ab, where are the paintings?' Husain said, 'They are coming by the next flight, Mishra sa'ab!' Mishra was horrified. 'But there is no next flight before the opening!' he wailed. Calmly, Husain replied, 'Come, let's go for dinner.'

The next morning, Husain met a forlorn Mishra. 'Shall we go to the gallery and see if the paintings are there?' he asked him. They walked in, and much to Mishra's delight, several large canvases were on display. It was a brilliant show. Later, Mishra saw that the paint on the canvas was still wet. Husain's paintings had not arrived in time. He had locked himself in his room and stayed up all night making new ones!

Husain finally made two big-screen movies, which he funded himself by selling his paintings. When he was eighty-one, a magazine published his paintings of Hindu gods. One of these was a nude, which he had painted in the 1970s. The image outraged many, and Hindu activists ransacked his home. Many of his paintings were burnt. Husain was forced to move to London and then Qatar, where he lived in self-exile.

Husain preferred to walk barefoot and was often turned away from hotels and clubs. When asked why he went without footwear, he said, 'Sages used to walk barefoot. It is good for health – like constant acupressure. It is also good for my knees, because I sit on them and paint for four to five hours at a stretch. In any case, people decide your status by seeing your footwear. Recognise me for who I am.'

VERGHESE KURIEN

MILKMAN OF INDIA

Verghese was annoyed. A few months ago, he had graduated with an engineering degree and was one of the lucky ten to have been selected to apprentice at the Tata Iron & Steel Company Limited (TISCO). What he didn't know was that his uncle John Mathai, a director at Tata, had pushed for his selection. When people came to know that he was Mathai's nephew, they started being extra nice to Verghese. He complained to his uncle, 'People are not taking me seriously. They are only taking *you* seriously!' Unhappy with the situation, Verghese rebelled and left.

Verghese wanted to study nuclear physics and metallurgy and applied to go abroad on a government scholarship. 'What do you know about pasteurisation?' the interviewer asked him. Verghese fumbled, and mumbled something about milk and sterilisation. 'Correct!' said the interviewer. He told Verghese that they would send him abroad for a degree in dairy engineering. Stunned, Verghese asked if he could get nuclear physics instead, but was told it was dairy or nothing.

When he finally got to Michigan State University, known for its department of dairy engineering, Verghese decided to study what he wanted, and attended only a few classes in dairy engineering. Armed with a master's degree with distinction, he headed home. In Delhi, he stayed with his uncle, who was now the finance minister of India.

Soon after, dressed in his natty style – a green shirt, yellow pants and a green felt hat – Verghese met the undersecretary of education for a job. The man looked Verghese up and down. 'You will have to report for work at Anand,' he said. Verghese asked, 'Anand? Where is that?' When he was told it was a small town in Gujarat, Verghese refused. But the official said, 'We have paid for your education. For the next five years, you have no choice but to work where we send you!'

An unenthusiastic Verghese was bored in the sleepy town of Anand. Every month, he sent his resignation letter to the ministry, and every month

Illustrated by Debangshu Moulik

it was refused. Tribhuvandas Patel, the head of the Kaira Cooperative, where Verghese worked, tried to keep the foreign-educated engineer busy. 'Dr Kurien, can you fix this machinery?' Verghese did what Patel asked, but he continued to send his resignation letters. One day, it was accepted. Verghese immediately packed up to leave. Patel came to meet him and said, 'Dr Kurien, don't go. Anand needs you.' Verghese had come to respect Patel, so he quietly unpacked his bags and stayed.

One challenge Verghese faced was the seasonal nature of milk supply. 'Buffaloes give more milk in winter, but people consume more in summer. How do I fix this?' Verghese went to New Zealand to understand how dairy cooperatives worked. He visited over a hundred plants and learnt how to make milk powder from milk. Back in India, he met the technical wizard of the dairy and his former Michigan classmate, H.M. Dalaya. Together, they cracked the challenge of making milk powder from buffalo milk. The sceptics said, 'What about the taste?' But when the minister of dairy had a taste, he declared it was just fine!

A year later, Prime Minister Nehru inaugurated India's first dairy plant – Amul.

Verghese knew that the key to increasing the demand for milk products was marketing. He asked Patel for money. 'Two lakh rupees? For advertising?' Patel was shocked, but Verghese convinced him. In 1966, Sylvester da Cunha and his team presented the cute mascot, 'Amul Girl', and the tagline 'The Taste of India'. Nisha da Cunha coined the line 'Utterly Butterly Delicious'. Dr Kurien said, 'Whatever does Butterly mean?' but he left the advertising to the experts. And what a success the campaign was!

Verghese went on to launch Operation Flood – to 'flood the market' with milk and connect rural farmers with consumers. He cut out the middleman to ensure more profit for the farmer.

Verghese was constantly at loggerheads with multinational companies, who believed they did things better than the Indians could. When he visited Nestle to ask them to manufacture condensed milk in India instead of exporting it, they said, 'Making condensed milk is a delicate procedure and we cannot trust the natives!' Verghese stormed out, and told Dalaya what had happened. They found a way for Amul to make condensed milk.

Then he wrote to the minister, asking for a ban on imported condensed milk. It was done!

Eventually, Amul also made and sold baby food powder. From being a country that was deficient in milk, India became the world's largest milk producer. All through these years of unmitigated success, Dr Verghese Kurien referred to himself as an employee of the dairy farmers of India.

SUNDERLAL BAHUGUNA

EARTH WARRIOR

Sunder was playing with his friends in Tehri when a man passed by, wearing a Gandhi cap and carrying a box. They were very curious. 'Is he a magician? What is in his box?' The man opened it and showed them a charkha, a spinning wheel. Then he showed them how to weave thread. He said, 'Gandhiji says that if all villagers spin their own yarn and make their own cloth, India can be free.'

The young man, Dev Suman, was a Gandhian. 'What will you do when you grow up?' he asked Sunder. 'I will be an official!' Sunder replied. The man said, 'But you will be serving British masters. Who will take care of the poor?' Over the next few months, Suman spent time with the boys, talking to them about freedom and revolution. Sunder began to save money and bought a charkha of his own to spin yarn.

When Suman was jailed for protesting against the oppressive ruler of the region, Sunder got word to the media. The police were befuddled. 'Who told the newspapers?' When they found out it was seventeen-year-old Sunder, they jailed him too. Sunder wasn't allowed to bathe for months. Sometimes they even mixed kerosene in his food! One day, Sunder got news that Suman had died. He was devastated and became terribly ill. The police called a doctor. Luckily, the doctor was a friend of Sunder's family and convinced the police to temporarily release Sunder into his care.

After being released, Sunder was quickly sent to Lahore, where he enrolled in an undergraduate course. Once, while walking home, he saw a policeman outside his room. 'Oh no, they are still looking for me,' he thought. Friends told him, 'Sunder, go far away, where the police cannot find you.' So off he went to a village called Sikhanwala. He even changed his name to S. Maan Singh. A grain merchant hired Sunder to tutor his children. Sunder taught the kids well. He lived austerely. He spun his own khadi and ate only one meal a day. When the police finally stopped looking for him, he went back to Lahore to finish his studies.

Illustrated by Adwait Pawar

By the time he went back to his beloved Tehri, much was happening there. He got involved in local issues of welfare and became a district leader of the Congress Party.

Sometime later, the government sold hundreds of ash trees in the forest to a factory for making sports equipment. When the villagers heard the news, they were angry. 'These trees are used by our cattle, our homes. We have to protect them.' Women from the village tied a 'rakhi' around the tree trunks and hugged the trees. They sang to the contractors who tried to scare them: 'Trees are not for resin and timber but for soil, water and pure air.'

Sunder was inspired by the courage of these women and decided to become a messenger for them. 'I need to tell people about the threat to our land.' So he and a few others – including the singer Ghanshyam Sailani – went on a padyatra, a long journey by foot, for 120 days, spreading the message. Sailani sang stories about the women, using the word 'chipko', meaning 'to cling', and soon villagers were talking about the Chipko Movement as a form of protest.

Yet, the felling continued. So, in true Gandhian style, Sunder went on a fast to protest. Finally, the chief minister met him, but he was angry. 'Sunder, the women are obstructing our work,' he said. Sunder replied, 'The trees are theirs.' He then met Prime Minister Indira Gandhi, who was in agreement with his views on the environment. Finally, the Uttar Pradesh government relented and gave orders to stop the felling of trees over a certain height. Sadly, the ban lasted only ten short years.

One day, Sunder came to know of a big dam being built in Tehri. 'The Himalayas are fragile, and this is an earthquake-prone zone. The ecology of the land will be destroyed! Villagers will be deprived of water!' He organised a cycle yatra, and young people spread the word about the hazards of building the dam. Sunder and his wife moved into a small hut near the site of the dam, to protest its construction. He fasted for forty-five days. But after ten years of resistance, they were forcibly moved away.

Sunder died in 2021 of complications caused by COVID-19. His advice to everyone was, says, 'If trees had a voice, they would tell you not to kill them. Before roti, kapda aur makaan, you need water and oxygen. Work towards saving those.'

Illustrated by Joanna Mendes

G. VENKATASWAMY

VISIONARY HEALER

Five-year-old Venkat skipped his way home from school, trying not to scald his bare feet on the hot sand. The village school in Vadamalapuram had no books or paper for the children to write on. So they improvised – writing with little sticks or their fingers on the wet river mud.

Not just schools, healthcare was vastly neglected in the village. One night, Venkat woke to the screams of a pregnant woman. In the morning, he overheard his mother saying of their neighbour, 'Poor thing, she died while having a baby.' In the next few years, three of his cousins also died due to complicated pregnancies. Venkat was sad. He thought, 'I will become a doctor when I grow up!'

When he was ten, Venkat's parents sent him to his uncle's house in Kovilpatti for a better education. Venkat had a skin condition called psoriasis. Because he always felt itchy and his skin was scaly and red, he found it hard to do his schoolwork. But he was determined to fulfil his childhood dream. Eventually, he finished both school and college, and got admission in a medical college in Chennai.

But luck was not on his side. His parents passed away soon after, and Venkat was left to take care of his four siblings including a five-year-old sister. Despite all the hardships, he graduated second in his class. In 1944, he joined the Indian Army as a medical officer. Once again, fate was cruel. At thirty, Venkat developed a condition called rheumatoid arthritis. His fingers and joints caused him great pain, and he could barely stand up. He had to stay in hospital for a year before he was well enough to leave. However, he was often treated terribly, especially in trains and in restaurants. His gnarled joints and skin condition made people think he had leprosy and they moved far away from him.

Venkat returned to medical college to specialise in gynaecology. There, senior doctors encouraged him to join the eye department instead.

Venkat knew that being an eye doctor meant being skilful and precise. He thought, 'The eye is so small and delicate. Will I be able to operate with my knobbly fingers?' He took it on as a challenge, trained hard and was soon using a scalpel proficiently.

Dr Venkataswamy (or Dr V, as he was popularly known) joined a government hospital in Chennai. The Tamil Nadu government wanted to hold mobile eye camps in rural areas. Remembering how poor the healthcare in his village was, Dr V took charge. He gathered his team and they went from village to village. Classrooms were the only spaces they could use. Dr V would roll up his sleeves and say, 'Let's move the furniture, sterilise the space and make a functional operating theatre to perform cataract surgeries.' Every day, they would start work at 5 a.m. and work till 7 p.m.

In 1965, Dr V met Sir John Wilson, a Blind British activist. The two got along famously. Sir John said, 'Dr V, you must work on bigger projects so that you can help even more people – hundreds of thousands!' Inspired, Dr V began working with the Indian government to establish a large-scale programme to help the visually impaired.

When Dr V retired, he asked his now successful siblings – whom he had educated and supported all his life – to help him set up an eyecare hospital. They came together and started the first not-for-profit hospital called 'Aravind Eye Hospital' in Madurai. From its initial eleven beds, the hospital grew to 330 beds. Dr V made sure that seventy per cent of the beds were reserved for the poor.

Once, while attending McDonald's Hamburger University for a few days, Dr V stood for hours watching how the team churned out burgers to a strict standard. From this, he figured out how to make the operations at his hospital faster. But even while trying to make things faster and better, Dr V never lost his human touch – his patients always came first.

Today, the Aravind eye-care system is a case study at the Harvard Business School. It has grown into a large hospital chain across South India. Despite his arthritic hands, in his lifetime Dr V performed over 100,000 surgeries himself – a true testament to his willpower.

ANANT PAI

STORYTELLER, ATHEIST

Anant and his sisters were attending a pooja at their grandparents' home. The priest was reciting the story of Satyanarayana: 'As soon as Kalavati finished the Satyanarayana prayer for her husband's release and came to know that he would be returning, she ran to meet him without taking the prasad. Angered by this, Satyanarayana drowned the boat in which her husband was coming back. God did this to teach her a lesson, never to forget to accept the pooja prasad with utmost respect.'

Anant was perplexed. How could God get angry over a little thing? He took the prasad after the ceremony and threw it in a ditch. His grandfather was horrified and sent him to the school headmaster to be punished. The headmaster asked Anant why he had thrown away the prasad. Anant said, 'My friend Sivanna pulled my hair in class the other day, and I forgave him. How come God, who is so great, can't forgive someone who forgot something?' The headmaster smiled and replied, 'Your logic is sound, son. But you must apologise to your grandfather because you have offended him.' Anant was lucky to have such understanding teachers in school.

When they were older, Anant and his sisters moved to Bombay to live with their cousins. No school wanted him since he didn't speak English. Finally, he did get admission, but the boys at school teased him for the way he spoke and looked. Anant ignored them and focused on his education – he loved studying and lapped up everything he read. When the results were announced, Anant stood first in class.

After finishing school, he was all set to become an engineer, but realised that his true passion was storytelling. He learnt everything he could about publishing and then joined the books division of a newspaper. There he discovered that publishers only wanted to market Western comics to kids. He now understood why Indian children knew more about Apollo and Medusa than their own mythologies.

Illustrated by Priya Kuriyan

He went to meet the Mirchandanis of India Book House. 'Why can't we make chitra-kathas or comic books with stories from Indian mythology?' he asked. They mulled over the idea and said, 'Let's try!' Anant excitedly wrote a few scripts and hired illustrators and researchers. He called his comics 'Amar Chitra Katha'. The first comic featured Lord Krishna and rolled out of press in 1970.

But who would do the marketing? No one knew about these Indian comics. Anant travelled by train all around the country to try and get booksellers to display them. Many of the sellers told him that they had no space. So he built little shelves in their shops so they could showcase his comics.

Once, while travelling by train, he was sharing a bogey with a bunch of kids and their parents. He 'accidentally' let his briefcase full of comics slip open. The curious children came to see and were soon engrossed in them. 'Where did you buy these?' some parents asked. Anant gave them the names of bookstores that stocked his comics.

Anant wanted his comics to be more interesting for kids than their drab history textbooks. And they were. Once, a school gave thirty children the comic *Sultana Razia*. Comics as textbooks? What fun! The students who read the comic passed their history exams with ease. This convinced other schools to add Amar Chitra Katha comics to their libraries.

Uncle Pai, as children used to call him, then started a comic digest called *Tinkle*, which sold all 35,000 copies of the first edition within a short while. He became one of the most successful publishers and marketers of children's writing in India. People from all over still collect Amar Chitra Katha comics.

While Uncle Pai had no children of his own, he and his wife Lalita considered every child who loved stories their own. He believed in Dale Carnegie's formula for success – 'Envision a goal, get busy and work hard.'

Illustrated by Sadhna Prasad

A.P.J. ABDUL KALAM

SCIENTIST TO PRESIDENT

Abdul was sitting with his best friend, Ram, in the front row of their classroom. A new teacher walked into the fifth grade. He took one look at Abdul and exclaimed, 'How dare you sit next to a Hindu! Go and sit on the back bench!' As Abdul walked away perplexed, he saw Ram crying. After school, both boys went home and told their parents what had happened. Ram's father was the high priest of the Rameshwaram temple. He summoned the young teacher and said, 'You are a teacher. How can you teach children to discriminate? Apologise now!' The teacher did and eventually changed his ways.

As a young man, Abdul studied at the prestigious Madras Institute of Technology (MIT). He was fascinated by the two decommissioned airplanes on the campus. 'I want to be a pilot someday,' he would tell his friends. After college, Abdul applied for two jobs, both of which involved working with planes – in the Indian Air Force and in the Ministry of Defence. He eventually went on to work at the Department of Defence.

Once, Abdul was working on a hovercraft project called Nandi. He was crushed when the project was shelved. But soon after, he had a visitor. The man asked Abdul some technical questions. Then he said, 'Will you show me how this works?' Thrilled with the man's interest in the project, Abdul gave him a ten-minute ride. They hovered only a few centimetres above the ground, since it was only a rudimentary prototype.

Shortly after the visitor left, Abdul was invited to join the Indian Committee for Space Research as a rocket engineer. There, he met the dynamic Vikram Sarabhai, who interviewed him. 'He has none of the arrogance that I have faced with other interviewers,' Abdul thought. 'And he is asking me exploratory questions instead of the usual technical ones.' Sarabhai had big plans. 'We are building India's first rocket, with NASA,' he said. Abdul was selected to be part of the team that eventually went to Thumba and successfully launched the rocket.

By 1973, Abdul Kalam was the mission director of the Satellite Launch Vehicle programme. The first satellite, SLV3, was ready to go to space. The computer started the test and four-minute countdown, but suddenly it stopped! The experts in the control centre did some quick calculations and reassured Kalam that it would be fine. So Kalam manually overrode the system and launched the satellite. But in the second stage of rocket separation, instead of going into space, the satellite fell straight into the Bay of Bengal. During the press conference, the chairman, Satish Dhawan accepted responsibility for the failure. Kalam was astounded, since it was the mission director's responsibility, not the chairman's – his failure, not Dhawan's.

A year later, the team launched another satellite – Rohini. Everyone waited with bated breath. This time, it was a success. There was much screaming and jubilation at the Sriharikota Range. Chairman Satish Dhawan told Kalam, 'You hold the press conference.' When Dhawan spoke to the media, he delightedly said, 'The hero of the day is Kalam – Abdul Kalam.' Kalam learnt an important management lesson in that moment, one that no book had ever taught him: in failure, leaders should assume responsibility; in success, they should credit their teams!

In 1989, Kalam and his team were ready to launch India's first missile – Agni. The world was watching. But at the last minute, they had to abort the mission for technical reasons. Not one to give up, Kalam rounded up his demoralised team. 'Years ago, I lost my launch vehicle to the Bay of Bengal. But we recovered it and made a success of it in a year. Your missile is in front of you. All you need is a couple of weeks of rework!' The team went back to work, re-energised.

One night before the launch, the defence minister asked Kalam, 'What would you like me to do to celebrate the success of Agni tomorrow?' Kalam said, 'We need 100,000 saplings to plant at Research Centre Imarat.' The minister was nonplussed.

It was a tense morning for all the scientists, but at 7.10 a.m., Agni took off to a textbook trajectory. It was one of the greatest moments of Kalam's life.

Abdul Kalam went on to become India's eleventh and most popular president. He would give his email address to students and ask them to send him an answer to this question: 'What will you be remembered for?'

E. SREEDHARAN

METRO MAN

Six-year-old Sreedharan was about to go on his very first train ride. At the station, he was transfixed by the big metal engine, the wooden bogey, the sound of the train and the smoke.

As a teenager, he moved to his sister's home to continue his studies. There he would sneak away to walk along the railway tracks and get a good, close look at the engines when they stopped.

Years later, when he graduated with an engineering degree, his brother said, 'Sreedharan, why don't you get a job in the Indian Railways? It is a prestigious place to be.' Although the Indian Railways Service of Engineers (IRSE) exam was tough, Sreedharan came seventh and joined the railways at twenty-two. He worked diligently and rose swiftly through the ranks.

In 1964, a cyclone hit Rameswaram Island and destroyed the Pamban Bridge, along with a train and all its passengers. To add to the tragedy, there was now nothing connecting Pamban and the mainland, which left thousands of people stranded. The chief engineer knew the man who could help and rang him up. 'Sreedharan, report to Madras immediately.' From there, they sent him to Rameswaram, giving him only three short months in which to complete the project!

When Sreedharan arrived in Pamban, he found that 126 girders from the bridge had been washed away. 'Three months?' he thought. 'This will be impossible to pull off even in six months! Even if I order new girders from Gujarat, they will take too long to get here. What can I do?'

Fortunately, some local fishermen came to him and said, 'We have seen old girders from the broken bridge under the sea.' Sreedharan got into a boat with them and they sailed out. Sure enough, about fifty kilometres from the coastline, when he peered through the crystal-clear waters, he saw many undamaged girders.

Illustrated by Aparajita Ninan

Elated, he told them, 'Locate all the girders for me.' He employed workers from the Mappila Khalasi community to pull out the girders. He had them cleaned, fixed, painted and assembled, after which the rail tracks were laid again. Forty-six days later, Sreedharan and his team flagged off the first train, much to everyone's amazement. The minister of Railways gave Sreedharan a cash award – the first of many he received. Soon after, he became a chief engineer in the railways.

When the Calcutta Metro was being planned, Sreedharan was assigned to build it. But planning a metro was a huge leap forward from the railways. How would he do this? He attended a conference in Japan, but that wasn't enough. 'I need to learn more,' he thought. 'Let me stay a few more days and work with the Japanese engineers here.' Despite the language barrier, Sreedharan used his engineering background to interpret models and scale-drawings. He returned to India, armed with a new confidence. Alas, Calcutta did not have the infrastructure and resources needed, and after four years, Sreedharan gave up the battle.

Life had even bigger plans for him, though. When the Delhi Metro Rail Corporation (DMRC) was formed in 1997, they needed a managing director. Everyone knew Sreedharan was the best person for the job. When the advisory committee asked him to come back from retirement he said, 'I want complete autonomy, and I want to choose my own team.' They readily agreed.

Once the project was launched, Sreedharan told his team, 'There are three principles we should follow. Quick decision-making, delegation of work to trusted people and using a reverse clock!' His team was bewildered. A reverse clock? What was that? Sreedharan said, 'Time is money. For every day the metro project gets delayed, we lose crores of rupees. Every office should have a clock that counts down backwards from the number of days each team has to finish one task.' And so, reverse clocks were installed in every office and the teams became more efficient.

During this time Sreedharan was often dejected because of interference by bureaucrats. He would then turn to his favourite text, the Bhagwad Gita, which inspired him to do his duty above all. He remained with the DMRC for sixteen years and delivered the first and second phases of a world-class metro.

Sreedharan tried his hand at politics, though unsuccessfully. He still works still works as an advisor for various projects in the country and lives in what he considers the most beautiful place in the world – Kerala.

Illustrated by Ayesha Broacha

T.N. SESHAN

INTEGRITY ABOVE ALL

Seven-year-old Seshan was staying up all night studying for his primary school Bible exam. 'Go to sleep, Raja, or you will fall asleep in the examination hall,' his mother warned him. But Seshan refused to listen. Next morning, he went to school confidently. In the exam hall, the teachers read out the questions, which the children had to write down on a sheet. They would then use another sheet to fill in the answers.

After the exam, when Seshan reached home, he realised he had carried back the answer sheet and submitted the question paper! He panicked, thinking he would fail and be detained for a year. That night, he and his father rushed to the headmaster's house. 'Will you please accept Seshan's answer paper?' his father asked anxiously. The headmaster replied, 'That is not possible. But you see, Bible studies is not a compulsory subject. So we are not going to detain Seshan.' Seshan thanked his stars and promised to heed his mother's advice in the future. From that night on, Seshan never studied for any test the night before.

When Seshan grew up, he wanted to study engineering. He had scored one hundred per cent in physics, chemistry and maths in his board exams and was confident he would be admitted. But during the admissions, an interviewer quizzed him endlessly about the film actor Sivaji Ganesan. Seshan found the process completely absurd. He wanted to join engineering, not the film industry! He ended up enrolling for a BSc and then an MSc in physics instead.

Years later, when he cleared his IAS exam, he was at the top of his class again. He rose through the ranks, serving in the Department of Atomic Energy, the Department of Space and the Defence Ministry, among others, until he became Cabinet Secretary. Along the way he rubbed many powerful people the wrong way with his outspokenness.

Once, on his first independent posting as an IAS officer, Seshan was in a car sitting between two ministers. A sarpanch who was related to a senior politician had been caught embezzling money. Seshan had ordered that action be taken and the sarpanch had been jailed. One of the ministers in the car said to Seshan, 'Seshan, I want you to withdraw your order.' But Seshan refused; he had done his duty according to the rules. The angry minister dropped him off in the middle of nowhere. Seshan stood under a tree for two hours in the hot sun until someone came to fetch him.

In 1990, Seshan was appointed the Chief Election Commissioner of India. During elections, most politicians used government facilities like air travel and spent huge amounts of money while campaigning. No one had any idea where this money came from. Seshan put the brakes on spending above the allowed limit. He boldly took on the central and state governments and got them to issue voter ID cards for every voter so that people did not vote on behalf of others. Political parties had also been ignoring the rules that were supposed to be followed during elections. Seshan pointed them to the Model Code of Conduct. They said, 'This is just a guideline, it is not the law. You cannot force us to follow it.' But Seshan implemented it all with the law and the constitution on his side. He even appointed senior officers as election observers to make sure that all guidelines were obeyed. In 1996, he conducted the cleanest elections in Indian history.

Seshan's biggest clashes were with Prime Minister Narasimha Rao, who was fed up of his unyielding ways. Rao once called Seshan to his office and said, 'I will give you whatever you want, but you must leave the Election Commission.' Seshan asked, 'What will you give me?' The prime minister replied, 'I'll make you a governor.' Seshan said, 'Sir, the only way I will become a governor is if my wife becomes a governess. We haven't found a suitable child yet.' Exasperated, Rao said, 'Fine, what about an ambassador?' Without missing a beat, Seshan retorted, 'I came in one.' He of course meant the car, while the prime minister meant the position of an ambassador. Rao walked away angrily.

Seshan didn't back down from any confrontation and was called 'Seshan the Alsatian' because he was like a watchdog everyone was scared of. Many said, 'Politicians fear only two things – God and Seshan.' When he was asked why, Seshan calmly replied, 'I never provoke people to make them afraid of me. I cherish my integrity. And that, for many, is scary.'

T. N. SESHAN

Illustrated by Sudeepti Tucker

RUSKIN BOND

BELOVED STORYTELLER

Ruskin was eating an orange when he accidentally swallowed a seed. His ayah said, 'Now an orange tree will grow inside your body, baba.' Ruskin was alarmed. He went to the cook, Osman, who used to tell him lots of stories. 'She is a gapori – don't listen to her!' Osman said. 'What's a gapori?' asked young Ruskin. 'Someone who makes up exaggerated stories.' Ayah ran after Osman till he said she was a pari, not a gapori!

Ruskin's life was filled with stories and adventure. But this changed when his father joined the Royal Air Force in Delhi. Ruskin and his mother went to Dehradun to stay with his granny. Granny was no fun; her constant refrain was, 'Little boys should only speak when spoken to.'

Soon, Ruskin was shipped off to his father in Delhi. The two had a grand time together. But then his father declared, 'It's time to send you to boarding school in Shimla.' Ruskin didn't want to go, but once there, he had a good time. Unlike his earlier boarding school, this one was fun!

Ruskin would tell his dad, 'When you come to visit me, wear your uniform.' His classmates asked, 'Does he fly bombers?' Ruskin would lie and say, 'Yes!'

At school, Ruskin discovered the library and broke straight into the world of detective stories and crime thrillers. When he visited his dad on vacations, they would watch musical films. Ruskin wanted to be a tap dancer and would practise for hours, while the staff stared at him in amusement. In the evening, the two would have tea with jam sandwiches and sort his father's stamp collection. Every day, Ruskin watched his father knocking his shoes on the floor before wearing them. He didn't know why, but he followed suit. One day, a centipede fell out of his shoe! That's when he realised what his father was doing.

Ruskin loved his father and shared a deep bond with him. Sadly, soon after he went back to boarding school, his father fell ill and passed away. Ruskin was devastated.

Back in school in Shimla, Ruskin made good friends with a boy called Azhar. When Ruskin began writing – short stories, poems, essays – Azhar encouraged him. But Ruskin wanted to be a sportsman. Azhar said, 'In sport one loses sometimes, you know. Better to be a writer!' After the Partition in 1947, Azhar had to leave for Pakistan. Ruskin was heartbroken, but they vowed to meet again.

When he finished school, Ruskin went to Dehradun, where his mother lived with her new family. He was given a barsati, a terrace room, with a typewriter, a chair and an earthen vessel for water. Here, Ruskin typed out his stories. A story called 'The Untouchable' was published in *The Illustrated Weekly of India*. Ruskin received a cheque for fifty rupees. 'I have arrived!' he thought.

After a while, Ruskin left for England. He looked around for a job. He would knock on doors and say, 'I can type, I can do math, I can play football.' He got some odd jobs as a clerk and even read some of his poetry on the radio. Finally, he heard from Diana Athill, an editor. She had read his manuscript, a novel called *The Room on the Roof*, which he had written at the age of seventeen. Ruskin was twenty-two, the book was published – his first novel! A year later, it went on to win a major prize.

Eventually, Ruskin moved back to India – first to Delhi and then to Mussoorie. His favourite pastime was walking – alone. He would observe people and talk to elderly women and tourists. He got himself some pets. Once, his cook came running. 'Bagheera Pickle *ko le gaya*!' The leopard had taken his dog – Pickle!

Ruskin met a young man, Prem, who took over his kitchen and cooked for years. When Prem got married, his wife joined the household. They took care of the home while Ruskin wrote. Ruskin would take Prem's son, little Rakesh, to school and tell him marvellous stories about a man-eating leopard. Then, Rakesh too got married and Ruskin became Da (grandfather) to not only Rakesh but also his children.

Ruskin kept writing all through these years. He was signed on by Penguin, the international publishing house, and several of his books were published – novels, short stories and poems.

The famous writer Ismat Chughtai once recommended Ruskin's book called *A Flight of Pigeons* to the director Shyam Benegal. Ruskin was paid ten thousand rupees, and it was made into a Hindi movie – *Junoon*.

At some point, Ruskin abandoned his typewriter and refused to use computers and technology. If he has to communicate with people, he sends them hand-written postcards.

Whenever he travels to cities for literature festivals, children throng the venues. Everybody loves Ruskin's stories.

Illustrated by Rae Zachariah

GIRISH KARNAD

ACTOR AND ACTIVIST

It was pitch black. There was no electricity in the jungle village of Sirsi. No electricity meant there was little to do at night. But Girish and his siblings had fun. Their parents would tell them stories till late into the night.

Sometimes, the family went to watch the Yakshagana dancers, who wore colourful headgear and face paint. Girish was fascinated by these performances. Through them, he learnt about history and the Puranas. Often, he would wander away from home to hang out with the actors and even learnt some acting from them.

When his father was transferred to Dharwad, Girish found himself at a loose end with not much to do. He started to sneak out of the house early in the morning to swim in the Someshwara temple tank. But Dharwad didn't remain boring for long. The city gave Girish an opportunity to mingle with great scholars like D.R. Bendre, Kirtinath Kurtakoti, G.B. Joshi and, later, A.K. Ramanujan. Their ideas about literature and poetry greatly influenced him.

Girish wanted to study abroad, but his father couldn't afford to fund him. 'I need a scholarship,' Girish thought. 'But if I study the subjects I like – Kannada, history and English – I won't be able to score a first class.' So he chose mathematics – a subject he hated. But it taught him rigour, logic and discipline. He stood first in class and was admitted to Oxford as a Rhodes Scholar to study what he enjoyed – philosophy, politics and economics. Girish wanted to be an English poet like T.S. Eliot and W.H. Auden and win a Nobel Prize someday.

But at home, there was chaos. Girish's parents couldn't afford to pay the fare for his sixteen-day journey by ship, to and from England every year. His parents were sad. 'Try and find a way to come back to India. Three years is very long,' they said. 'What if you marry a foreigner?' Girish felt as though he was in a scene from the Ramayana, with Yayati demanding that Puru sacrifice his youth for him. A story began to form in his head, which he hastily penned down in Kannada, in the form of a play. He called it 'Yayati' and gave it to G.B. Doshi, who promised to read it.

Once at Oxford, Girish immersed himself in life there. He became president of the Oxford Union and met with a number of politicians. Meanwhile, he got a letter from Kurtakoti, telling him to re-write 'Yayati'. Girish did, and when he was twenty-two, the play was published. People loved his writing. That's when he knew he wanted to come back to India. 'I don't want to be an English poet,' he decided. 'I want to be a Kannada playwright!'

On his way back to India, he read the story of Mohammad bin Tughlaq. 'This is marvellous,' he thought. 'A mad king who banned public prayers in his kingdom for five years? A king who went against his priest and against the Quran? This will make a fantastic play!' And Girish immediately got down to writing the story of Tughlaq. By the time he reached Bombay, he had the first draft ready. And what a success the play was!

Over the years, Girish wrote and directed many powerful plays. He also wrote screenplays and acted in movies. He made his film debut in *Samskara*, a powerful attack on the caste system in India. He also wrote on mythology, folklore, historical figures, contemporary subjects – his repertoire was astounding. When he was thirty-five, he took over as the youngest director of the Film and Television Institute of India (FTII). Some of his students were even older than him!

Always honest and outspoken, Girish managed to ruffle many feathers with his political statements. He spoke against religious hatred and intolerance, which was gaining momentum in India. Over the years, all this took a toll on his health and, in 2019, he succumbed to a severe respiratory illness.

When Girish attended journalist Gauri Lankesh's first death anniversary in 2018, it was with an oxygen cylinder and a tube connected to his nose. He wore a placard around his neck that said, 'Me Too Urban Naxal'.

ROMULUS WHITAKER

SNAKE MAN

Romulus loved looking for creepy-crawlies at his aunt's estate in New York. On one of his quests, he caught a garden snake. Rom was fascinated by the creature and ran to show it to his mother. 'Wow! How beautiful!' Doris exclaimed. She approved of her son's lively interest in animals and bought him his first book about snakes.

Doris moved to Bombay when Rom was nine. She sent her son to a boarding school in Tamil Nadu. Once, while visiting his mother on vacation, he saw a python being sold in the market. Rom scrimped and saved and managed to buy it. But soon, he had to go back to school. Now what? He put the python in his backpack and carried it with him on the train. In the hostel, Rom kept the bag under his bed. 'Snakes are perfect pets,' he thought. 'Always calm.'

When Rom went back to Bombay for his holidays, he took his python along. One day, when he looked in the cage, he found the python missing. After searching everywhere without luck, he reluctantly paid his neighbour a visit. 'Excuse me ... my pet is missing. It is a python – not large, only about five feet or so. It likes cool spots. Perhaps it is in your bathroom?' His neighbour was horrified! Still, he went to the bathroom to check. When he came out, he was frowning. 'It doesn't seem to be here, but please tell us when you find it!' Dejected, Rom went back to his apartment. This time, when he looked around again, he found the python in the storeroom under some trunks. (Snakes love dark, cosy places!) Rom quickly informed his spooked-out neighbour that the python was at home and back in its cage.

After Rom finished school, he enrolled in a college in the US. But he did not really enjoy studying and dropped out within a year. He landed a chance to work with the legendary Bill Haast, the director of the Miami Serpentarium Laboratories. There, he learnt how to look after snakes and extract their venom. Thousands of people visited the serpentarium and

Illustrated by Shantanu Sharma

the snake farm. Rom realised that even though people were scared of snakes, they were still interested in learning about them. 'I'll go back to India and open a snake park there!' he decided.

In 1969, Rom went back to Tamil Nadu to live with the Irulas – a tribe of snake catchers – who taught him how to find snakes. He eventually settled near Madras, in a place that was full of snake pits spread over acres of land. Here, he opened a snake park. Before long, people were visiting in the hundreds.

One day, the Chief Conservator of Forests of the state said to Rom, 'Your park is so far away. We have a deer park in the city, and we can give you some space there to run it so that more children can visit.' 'Thank you!' Rom replied. He was happy with this offer and moved his snakes. At the same time, he continued to breed crocodiles at the snake park with Zia, his first wife. It became home to 2,300 crocodiles of more than seventeen species over the next forty years.

Once, in Australia, Rom spotted a snake crossing a highway in the middle of heavy traffic. He was on a film shoot, but stopped everything and zipped over to the snake. With his bare hands, he flipped it across the road to safety. But in the chaos, the snake sunk its teeth into Rom's thumb. Rom decided to catch the snake to see whether it was venomous. He chased it down, caught it and pried its mouth open to find two fangs. It was a Papuan Whipsnake – poisonous, but not deadly. He released the snake and decided not to go to the hospital since the injury was not fatal. He simply hid the swelling from the camera and refused to shake anyone's hand.

Rom says 60,000 people die of snakebites every year because they don't receive treatment in time. And when they do, it is often the wrong one. Today, Rom is helping scientists improve anti-venoms. He teaches people about snakes – how these creatures can be helpful to humans by eating pesky rodents, how one can avoid them, and that many local remedies for snakebite treatment are actually useless!

When asked if he names his snakes, Rom laughs and says, 'What's the point of naming them? They can't hear if you call them anyway.'

Illustrated by Sujata Bansal

AZIM PREMJI

PHILANTHROPY FIRST

Azim was at Haji Ali, watching his mother working hard at the children's orthopaedic hospital she had founded. She wanted to improve the lives of children who had polio and other disabilities. India had just become independent and there were many challenges facing the new nation. But Dr Gulbanoo Premji was unstoppable!

In the evenings, she would come home and tell her children stories about her day. She was raising funds for her charity and needed help from the government. Even when the money was sanctioned, she would have to keep following up to have it transferred. She worked fifty-sixty hours a week, all the while taking care of her own four kids at home. Her struggle and commitment to changing people's lives stayed with Azim.

As a young man, Azim went to Stanford. Even though he was there for a degree in electrical engineering, he took classes in history and also studied Shakespeare. He played tennis and joined an 'eating club', where students ate with each other and not at the cafeteria.

One day, the twenty-one-year-old was given the sad news of his father's demise. Azim's family wanted him to return home and take over his father's company – Western Indian Vegetable Products (WIPRO). So, Azim headed back to Bombay, with no experience of ever having worked in the business.

WIPRO manufactured cooking oil called Sunflower Vanaspati and also made laundry soap as a by-product of oil manufacturing. At his first shareholders' meeting, Azim was told, 'You won't be able to run such a complex company. You should consider selling your shares.' Rather than getting discouraged, Azim bought some business books and spent time studying and immersing himself in the day-to-day business. Soon, he was on top of everything and the company began diversifying. They began to sell baby and healthcare products. Then, WIPRO procured technology and launched a personal computer. It also set up a software research and development division.

IBM was WIPRO's big competitor in the computer market. In 1978, the Indian government accused IBM of selling obsolete equipment and told them to leave the country. Suddenly, there was an opportunity in the market! Azim and his team at WIPRO acted immediately.

Azim said to himself, 'We need to build a larger team. People are the most valuable assets. As a company, we must articulate our values and practise them without deviation!' He would personally interview people – sometimes for hours on end. Despite being the chairman of a now super-successful company, Azim would only travel economy class and owned a basic sedan. The company grew and WIPRO reached over fifty countries through business expansion.

In 2001, Azim transferred some of his shares worth 1.25 million dollars to set up a charitable organisation called the Azim Premji Foundation. The foundation works towards enhancing public education in rural India. He then added shares worth a couple of billion dollars in 2013 to the foundation. On top of this, in 2019, Azim made the single-largest donation by an Indian, transferring 7.5 billion dollars to the Foundation for various philanthropic initiatives. He was lauded globally.

'Philanthropy happened late for me,' says Azim. 'If one has been fortunate enough to have gotten much more than normal wealth, it is but natural that one has a fiduciary responsibility to put it to good use, for the benefit of society. I have always felt it is the right thing to do in a country with so much poverty, where people are so majorly disadvantaged. Unfortunately, wealthy Indians don't give like the Americans. For one, our families are much larger. The second reason is that the majority of wealthy Indians believe that they must leave their inheritance in its entirety to their children. I believe a sense of charity should be inculcated in every Indian, early in life.'

It is this willingness to give that sets Azim Premji apart from all the others.

MURLIKANT PETKAR

CHAMPION AGAINST ODDS

'Chotu, get me a glass of thandai.'

Ten-year-old Murli was grinding dry fruit to add to milk. Wrestling was the major sport in Murli's village. Being the youngest at the akhada, he was tasked with making the chilled drink. In return, he got to learn wrestling from his guru, Ganpat Rao Khedkar – and drink thandai. Soon, he was strong and muscular himself.

A neighbouring village held a mela where wrestling matches took place. The reward was not money but a batasha and a coconut. Once, the village head's muscular son – about as old as Murli – was ushered into the pit. The organisers announced, 'Whoever can defeat him will win prize money of one rupee.' When no one came forward, the prize was increased to two rupees. But everyone knew that if they fought him, they would have to lose. How could they beat the village headman's son?

The prize money was finally increased to five rupees. Murli asked Khedkar, 'Shall I go and try?' Khedkar nodded. Murli said, 'He is a little taller and my equal in training. What should I do?' Khedkar said, 'Murli, don't be afraid. Hold your ground.' The match was intense, and the villagers merrily threw money into the kitty. In the end, Murli picked up his opponent and threw him down. He had won!

Some people were furious that Murli had defeated the headman's son. They wanted to beat him up. Khedkar grabbed Murli's prize money, gave him twelve rupees from it, and put him on a truck. He paid the driver to take him away to Poona. There, Murli went to his aunt and uncle. When they heard his story, they said, 'Murli, it may not be safe for you to go home yet.' They saw an advertisement for the Boys' Battalion of the army, and Murli applied. There, he learnt to box and began to contest at the national level. He earned the name 'Chottu Tiger'!

Illustrated by Shruti Anand

In 1964, Murli was on his way to Japan for an international sports meet. At the cafeteria, he used cutlery for the very first time. He pressed down so hard with his fork and knife that he broke seven plates!

He won the silver medal at the tournament. The Boys' Battalion was very proud of him. 'What do you want, Murli?' his officers asked. 'Sir, I have never visited Kashmir. Please send me there,' he replied.

In Kashmir, Murli's troops were near the Indo-Pak border. He was at the barracks when he heard a whistle. 'It's teatime,' he thought. Murli never drank tea, so he didn't step out. But the whistle was actually a signal alerting the troops of air raids. When Murli ran out to the deafening roar of aeroplanes, he was shocked to see the dead bodies and bloodied limbs of his friends. The Indo-Pak war of 1965 had broken out!

During the war, Murli took nine bullets in his thigh, leg, spine and eye! He fell from a height to a road below, where a truck ran over him, leaving him in agony. Eventually, the Red Cross rescued him and moved him to a hospital in Delhi. He lost his memory for nearly seventeen months. He was also paralysed waist down. While the doctors managed to remove most of the bullets, one remained stuck in his spine.

The army later moved Murli to a hospital in Bombay. He was advised to swim to regain the strength in his legs. His family, however, refused to have anything to do with him. His brother said, 'You are disabled. We have no one to take care of you. You will be a burden on us.' His mother kept crying, but they walked away, leaving Murli all alone.

The commander of the hospital encouraged Murli to participate in international swimming meets and competitions. Murli had now become stronger and even more determined. By 1970, he'd won three gold medals in swimming, a silver in javelin throw and a bronze in shot put.

In 1972, at the Paralympics in Heidelberg, the crowds were rooting for the brave Indian soldier. Murli swam the fifty-metre freestyle and won India's first Paralympic gold medal! As the Indian flag went up, tears streamed down Murli's face. 'I may not have killed an enemy soldier, but I've won an Olympic gold for my country!'

When he landed in Bombay, he was whisked away to Colaba where almost 3,000 soldiers gave him a standing ovation. He was also flown to Delhi to meet Field Marshal Sam Manekshaw.

One day, industrialist J.R.D. Tata met Murli. 'How can I help you?' Tata asked. Murli, who had decided to leave the forces by then, said, 'I don't want any cash or land from you. Please give me a job. I want to be self-reliant.' Tata hired him on one condition – that Murli should continue to participate in competitions!

Sadly, Murli didn't get the national recognition he deserved in his competitive years. India hadn't yet started keeping records of Paralympic events.

Now married with children, Murli says, 'Destiny has been both cruel and kind to me. I was hit by nine bullets, but I also won a gold medal. Best of all, I am now surrounded by people who love me.'

GANESH DEVY

LANGUAGE IS LIFE

Six-year-old Ganesh walked out of his classroom and saw people reading books that had peacock feathers sticking out from between the pages. Ganesh didn't know what a bookmark was; he just loved the touch and feel of the bright blue feathers. 'Wow,' he thought dreamily. 'Books have peacock feathers in them!' Excited, he went to the library. He opened some books – no feathers. What jumped out at him instead were words, pictures and some wonderful stories. The librarian said he could borrow the books free of cost. So Ganesh picked up a few Marathi translations of Greek classics and rushed home to read them.

Ganesh loved science and maths. But in college, the way the teachers taught these subjects made no sense to him. 'Maybe my English isn't good enough because it is my third language,' thought Ganesh. Dejected, he caught a train to Goa and worked there as a labourer for a few months.

One day, he found a small library near his home. He borrowed *The Good Earth* by Pearl S. Buck and then read R.K. Narayan's *The Guide*. He realised he could indeed read and understand English. 'I am going to read three hundred pages a day, every day,' he decided. And he did! Now confident, Ganesh decided to return to college, this time to study English Literature. He went on to get an M.A. and a Ph.D.

Ganesh then became a Fellow at Leeds University. He thought, 'My favourite cricketer Geoffrey Boycott is from there. Maybe I'll get a chance to meet him.' Sadly, he couldn't meet Boycott, but came back in a year, armed with a second master's degree, after which he and his wife moved to Baroda to teach.

After some years, they shifted to the village of Tejgadh. Ganesh found the village life, the people, their languages and rituals highly sophisticated. He would sit for hours watching the villagers in the fields. 'There is wisdom in everything they do,' he thought. When they sowed seeds, they scattered them by splaying out their hands in a certain pattern. This helped the

Illustrated by Sudeepti Tucker

seeds grow better. Till now, he had only seen urban farmers forcing seeds into a rigid line.

'I am not here to tell people what to do,' Ganesh told himself, 'but to encourage them to do more of what they already do.' He documented the work of the tribal people. Their history, their folklore, their use of the land, how they cared for the environment, their medicine, music, arts and theatre. Before he knew it, tribal people from all over the country were visiting him. So he started the Bhasha Adivasi Academy to document the various tribes and their unique ways of living. Luminaries like Mahasweta Devi and Bhupen Hazarika would visit and stay there for months.

But when the data from the 1971 Census was released, Ganesh was infuriated. He thought, 'The 1961 Census showed that India had 1,652 mother tongues. Now, only 109 languages are listed. This means 1,543 languages have been suppressed! Why do tribal people have to learn new languages?' Ganesh felt that the government should protect all languages. But since they didn't seem to care, he decided to do something about it.

Ganesh called friends from all over the country and formed a team of 3,000 people. They started the People's Linguistic Survey of India. Together, they documented over 700 languages – along with their history, the songs and stories of the region, and even translations of important texts. They published their findings as a series of books. So far, they have published sixty books.

At forty-two, Ganesh received an award for his book *After Amnesia*. He stopped reading his quota of three hundred pages a day after that and focused on his research. When asked why, he replied, 'If a book speaks to me in five minutes of reading it, only then do I continue. But that is rare.'

In 2015, his friend and scholar M.M. Kalburgi was shot dead. 'The idea of India is being destroyed,' Ganesh thought, 'I cannot sit back any longer.' Ganesh and his wife moved to Dharwad to fight a legal battle for Kalburgi. He even returned his Sahitya Akademi Award in protest against the community that refused to condemn this dastardly attack.

Ganesh now spends his time finding ways for excluded communities to be included, and hopes to publish all ninety-one volumes of his work in the next few years.

Illustrated by Adwait Pawar

NASEERUDDIN SHAH

ACTORS' ACTOR

'Bye, Ammi,' said Naseer, as he and his friend Girish cycled away in their cricket whites. His school in Ajmer got over by 1.30 p.m., but they wanted to catch a movie. The only way they could do so on weekdays was to lie about having after-school cricket practice. The school screened some movies too, but the projector was rickety and the sound terrible. Besides, who cared about mythology? He wanted Dara Singh! He wanted King Kong!

One day, Naseer saw a bright red jeep pull up at school. Out jumped a jovial, red-faced man. Naseer stood open-mouthed when he saw who it was. 'It's Geoffrey Kendal. I've seen him perform Shakespeare's plays at my previous school, and he is as good as the actors on screen.' He leapt to the jeep and offered to unload the luggage. After he had taken it all excitedly to the auditorium, Kendal said, 'That will be all, thank you.' Naseer was stupefied. 'He shook my hand. Maybe I can convince him to let me join his troupe,' he thought.

After Kendal had performed *Gems from Shakespeare*, Naseer went backstage with his autograph book. He wanted to talk to the giant of an actor. Kendal quietly signed his book. In that moment, Naseer made up his mind. 'I must do something with my life!'

He soon took to acting in school plays. 'This is where I belong,' he thought. Teachers started noticing the young man who could act so well. Naseer grew more confident and went from being a wallflower to the 'best actor' in school.

When Naseer went to college, his heart wasn't in academics. He took a train to Bombay and stayed with friends while looking for a job. He was only sixteen years old. Once, when he was hanging around outside a restaurant, a man said to him, 'Come to the studio tomorrow morning. We need extra junior artistes.' Naseer thought, 'This is my big break!' But all he did was act as an extra.

Dejected, Naseer was sitting on the pavement one day, when a car pulled up. Out stepped an immaculately dressed woman. 'Are you Naseer?' she asked. He nodded, and she told him to get into the car. He realised then that she was the famous actor Dilip Kumar's sister, Sakina! She had stayed at their home a couple of times, while visiting the dargah in Ajmer. Naseer's father had requested Sakina to find him.

They drove to her house on Pali Hill. Sakina said he could stay a few days, but he had to go home to his parents after that. While he was there, Naseer saw Dilip Kumar. He tentatively approached him one day, when he was sitting in the garden. Dilip turned to him nonchalantly and said, 'Boys from good families should not take up acting.' And so, disheartened, Naseer went back home.

Eventually, Naseer did join the National School of Drama where he met a wonderful teacher, Ebrahim Alkazi. Until now, theatre had been fun – wigs, costumes and all. Alkazi taught the students the importance of discipline, and Naseer learned that one has to think of acting as a profession. So off he went to the Film and Television Institute of India (FTII). 'The fee is six hundred rupees. How will I pay?' With much trepidation, he shot off a telegram to his father, asking for the money. 'You will study this bloody acting for five more years? Might as well have become a doctor!' said his father. But he sent the money anyway.

The director of FTII was the famous playwright and actor Girish Karnad. One day, he told Naseer, 'You did a marvellous job in the play *Zoo Story*, Naseer. Shyam Benegal is casting for his next film, and I have recommended you. Leave for Bombay as soon as you can!' Naseer was selected and promised the princely sum of ten thousand rupees. This was his first film role; the film was called *Nishant* and had many stalwarts from the industry.

Naseer went on to act in over a hundred films and continues to do theatre. He says, 'There are some movies that you feel like doing because of the script. Some because they sound like fun, some because of the director, and some because one will be paid lots of money. But for me, the bottom line is that I must feel like doing it.'

ABHAY BANG

BEING THE CHANGE

Abhay was walking dejectedly among the brinjal plants he had sown in his school garden in Wardha. They weren't growing well. He went to his teacher and asked him what to do. 'Go read some botany,' he said. Abhay read that plants needed nitrogen to grow faster. 'How do I give my plants nitrogen?' he asked the teacher. 'Go read your chemistry,' he replied. Then Abhay read that urea contains nitrogen. He ran to the cowshed, where they stored cow's urine, and poured buckets of it on his plants every day. His plants grew to a great height of eight feet while Abhay was all of four feet! The biggest brinjal from these plants weighed 1.75 kg! When he proudly tried to sell it, people refused. 'It's too big. We will be eating brinjal all week!' In that year, Abhay felt he had learned planning, chemistry, botany, economics and marketing!

One day his brother Ashok said, 'Abhay, we should decide what to do in life.' The two looked at the farmers working hard in their fields. Ashok said, 'We need to improve agriculture and health in the villages. I'll focus on agriculture.' Thirteen-year-old Abhay replied, 'Fine, then I'll improve their health.' And that was how he decided to become a doctor.

While studying at the medical college in Nagpur, Abhay realised that he was getting accustomed to the comforts of city life. 'How will I work in a village if I get used to all this?' So, even on the hottest day, Abhay refused to use a fan, because there would be none in the villages.

Abhay married his classmate Rani – also a doctor – and together, they opened a clinic in Kahnapur village. Many of the villagers were suspicous. Why would two smart urban doctors come to their remote village? Still, they started visiting the clinic for treatment.

Abhay discovered that landless labourers in the area were paid a measly four rupees a day. He did some research and, based on that, appealed to

Illustrated by Shikanth Sablania

the state government to increase the minimum wage to twelve rupees. After a whole year of discussion and debate, the law was finally changed. That's when Abhay realised the importance of data and research. He and Rani then decided to study public health research at the Johns Hopkins School in the US.

On their return in 1986, the couple went to live and work in the tribal district of Gadchiroli. When they asked, 'What are your biggest health problems? How can we help?' the people said, 'We don't like you doctors!' 'Why?' asked Abhay. They replied, 'We cover our dead bodies with white cloth. When we see you in your white coats, we feel you are inviting death. And your hospitals are big and scary!' From that day, Abhay, Rani and the team stopped wearing white. They constructed a hospital campus that looked like a tribal village instead of an urban building. The villagers were happy and said, 'This is our hospital.'

While working there, Abhay realised that there were too many instances of infant mortality in the village. Pregnant women didn't eat well because they thought their babies would become too big and they would have trouble delivering. New mothers refused to come to the hospital even if their babies were sick because they thought, '*Bacche ko nazar lag jayegi.*' (An evil eye will be cast on the baby.) They also believed that the first yellowish milk from the mother, which looked like pus, was bad for the baby, when in fact, it was essential for the baby's health.

Abhay trained local women to be health workers and entrusted them with the care of newborn babies in the community. Over the years, he and his team managed to significantly reduce the number of infant deaths. The programme was so successful that it went global.

Abhay and Rani have now started Nirman, a programme where young Indians work in villages. Abhay's message to the youth is: 'Go where the problems are to solve them, and not where the facilities are and you are not needed.'

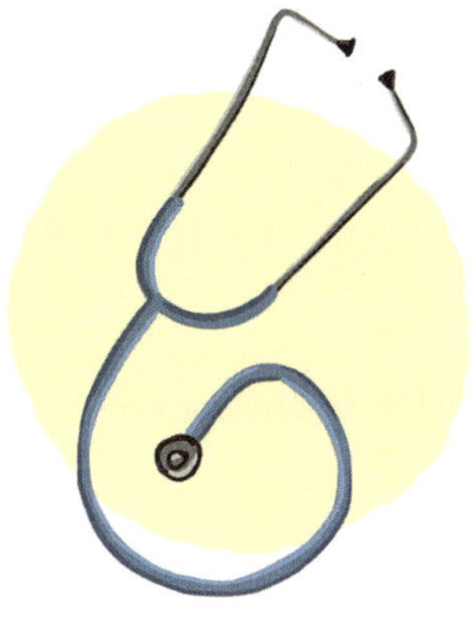

Illustrated by Shruti Anand

VIKRAM SETH

WORDSMITH

As a toddler, Vikram was told by his Nani to speak only in Hindi. So that was what they spoke at home. And then at age two-and-a-half he was sent to England, to be with his parents who had moved there. Forget speaking, Vikram had never even heard a word of English before. And there he was, plunged into an 'English only' environment. But by the age of four, he was speaking the Queen's English. A few years later, the shy and introverted boy was sent to a boarding school in Dehradun, a two-day train journey from home in Calcutta. Vikram didn't like being away from home. He moved to another boarding school, which was worse. He was bullied by senior students for being too short, too studious, for not participating in sports and not being part of a 'gang'.

At eighteen, Vikram was off to Oxford for a degree in philosophy, politics and economics. Classes were few and far between, so he took long walks and began to write poetry. After graduation, he moved to Stanford for a Ph.D. in economics. Once, at a friend's home, he read a book of poems by the Chinese poet Wang Wei. 'It would be wonderful to read these in the original,' he thought. He came up with an obscure topic for his Ph.D. thesis and went off to Nanjing University.

In China, he found that even though he had studied the language, he had trouble grasping the tonal variations. So, when someone asked him how he came to China, instead of saying 'by aeroplane', he ended up saying 'fat chicken'! But as he began reading poetry in Chinese, his skills improved. After two years, he decided to hitchhike his way back home to India via Tibet. Little was known about China then, so people constantly asked him about his adventures. His father said, 'Why don't you just write about your experience, Vikram?' And so, his first book was published – a travelogue.

When he returned to Stanford, Vikram wanted to work on being a creative writer. A year later, he wrote a novel called *The Golden Gate* – in verse. But the book he really wanted to write was an expansive novel set in India between the 1950s and 1990s. He knew that it would require research and time to write, and it was tough earning a living abroad. So he went back to his parents' home. 'You can stay with us, eat with us, and in the evening, you and your father can have a glass of whisky together,' said his mother, who was now a judge. The family lived in Noida in Uttar Pradesh.

Vikram began his painstaking research. He loved to sit on his bed, propped up on pillows, and write. He would wake up at noon and write for ten to sixteen hours. He wrote in longform, then moved to a laptop, then dictated notes to a friend, and finally moved back to writing by hand. He wrote this way for eight years, and his hand would often get cramped. Finally, his almost 600,000-word-long 'doorstop of a novel', *A Suitable Boy*, was ready to be published.

Giles Gordon, Vikram's agent, held an auction for the longest novel ever written. It was even longer than *War and Peace*! Nine publishers made a bid for it. On the day of the auction, a nervous Vikram arrived in Giles' office. 'Go away Vikram, you're getting in my way,' Giles said to him. So Vikram went and sat under a fig tree in the garden and eventually went home. The next day, Giles called Vikram. 'I've sold your book,' he said. Vikram said, 'You can't do that without my approval!' Giles said, 'I've sold it for a quarter of a million pounds.' Orion had bought the rights. It was the largest advance ever paid for a novel.

Vikram went on to write a number of novels including *An Equal Music*, which was dedicated to his then partner – a musician named Phillipe Honoré. Vikram was openly bisexual. When his mother was writing her autobiography, she asked him if it was all right to mention his orientation. Vikram believed that 'biographies should be full of not only things that are hard to write about but also those that give ordinary people courage'. So he replied, 'Of course, Mama! Anything that's important in your life should come up.'

Vikram is a polymath. He writes, sculpts, sings Schubert, is skilled at Chinese calligraphy and speaks multiple languages. In his heart, he considers himself a poet first and foremost. He says, 'Poetry is so dear to me that even in every prose book that I write, I somehow manage to wriggle in a poem at the beginning by way of a dedication.'

ANAND GROVER

LAWYER, CRUSADER

Young Anand was studying biochemistry in England but his heart was in India, which was in the midst of a political Emergency. He thought, 'I have scrimped and saved enough money. Let me go back to India and see how I can help.' So he flew to Bombay to volunteer with the Socialist Party. With them, he visited jails, bringing political prisoners food and clothing.

At the Workers' Law Centre, an NGO, he met the fiery lawyer Indira Jaising. Two things happened. The two fell in love and got married. And Anand realised he wanted to study law. He thought, 'Even in the middle of the Emergency, when nothing seems possible, law can bring change.' So he joined the Bombay Law College.

In 1987, Dr Ishwar Gilada from Goa asked Anand for help. He said, 'I have a patient whom the Goan government has put in jail. You know why? Because he is HIV positive!' At the time, people did not know much about HIV, so Anand learnt all he could from experts. Gilada stressed, 'This is not just a medical case, Anand. This is about discrimination. It is a human rights issue!'

Anand went to Goa to meet his client, who had just been released after sixty-four days of forced isolation. He asked him to wait in his hotel room. When he entered, he saw Dominic lying on his bed. Anand thought, 'Oh no, why is this HIV patient lying on my bed?' He immediately caught himself. 'Why did I react this way? I know that HIV cannot spread in this manner. How can I represent Dominic? I need to change my own thinking!' This was the first known case of HIV in India. Even though he lost the case, Anand managed to prevent the nationalisation of the draconian law that allowed incarceration of HIV patients.

A few years later, Anand received a call from Dominic's friend. 'Dominic is dying. He is at Breach Candy Hospital. Come and meet him.' Anand

Illustrated by Adwait Pawar

could barely recognise Dominic. Once an energetic theatre actor, he was now skin and bones. Dominic said, 'Anand, promise me that you will continue to work for HIV patients.' Without a second thought, Anand agreed.

Anand's big win for HIV patients came in 1998. He fought for their right to get government jobs, as long as they were fit and there was no significant risk of transmission. That's also when Anand and Indira started the Lawyers Collective. Their mission was simple – to serve those who were excluded by the system and needed legal services.

Soon, people from the LGBTQ+ community began approaching him. 'People we go on dates with blackmail us. Sometimes even the police threaten us and use violence. We cannot live our lives like this,' one person after another told him. Anand fought a historic case on behalf of the NAZ Foundation, to decriminalise gay sex. Fortunately, more people had started talking about LGBTQ+ rights. Eight years later, in 2009, Anand and the Naz Foundation won the battle, and the Delhi High Court decriminalised homosexuality.

The LGBTQ+ community celebrated. But it didn't last long. The apex court set aside the Delhi High Court's decision and restored Section 377. Anand tried his best to appeal to the court. 'Even one per cent of society can invoke fundamental rights,' he said. But it was futile.

A full nine years passed before the law was read back again, in 2018.

Anand also fought for equal access to medicines for all, regardless of class or sexual orientation. Here, his background in biochemistry helped him. Once, when a large pharmaceutical company wanted to patent its cancer medicine in a different form and increase the price, Anand took them on and won the case.

One day, one of Anand's junior lawyers came to him to discuss a case. Anand noticed that a document was missing. The junior lawyer said, 'Why don't we make it up?' Anand exploded. 'If you ever do that in my office, you will be kicked out! Lawyers are paid for using their brains and finding solutions – not for lying!'

Anand has always tried to bring about a positive change in people – himself included. One day, his accountant dropped in at his house for some signatures. Anand asked him to come in. The man refused. 'I am from a lower caste, I'll stand outside,' he said. Anand was outraged. The very next day, he changed things at the office. Now, everyone had to sit at the same table for lunch.

Anand says, 'All of us keep pretending we believe in equality, but equality begins when your household staff sit and eat at the same table as you do!'

ARVIND GUPTA

LEARNING WITH TOYS

Arvind looked proudly at the collection of matchboxes and old cigarette packets that he had amassed. 'Look, Ammaji! Now I have enough stuff to make something.' He put the boxes together to make a cardboard house.

Arvind knew he had to make do with what was available, since his parents could not afford toys. His mother had sold all her jewellery just so she could send her children to the best school in Bareilly.

One day, their uncle brought them a gift. It was a Meccano set! When his elder brother and sister were done playing with it, Arvind delightedly pulled out the green, red and yellow plastic strips, girders and axles. With the help of the instruction pamphlet, he powered through easily. Soon he was making original models.

At school, Arvind's teacher Mrs Frey made maths fun. She would use paper models that they would cut and fold. Very little theory – and a lot more hands-on stuff. But while Arvind was great at maths, his English wasn't good. So Mrs Frey would speak to him only in English and often told him, 'Arvind, I have faith in you.' Eventually, Arvind became more confident and passed his English exams with honours.

Arvind studied for the Indian Institute of Technology (IIT) exam. He couldn't afford the expensive coaching institutes, so his sister helped him study. After the exam, he told his sister how he had fared. She went to their mother and said, '*Ammaji, Arvind IIT pahunch* jayega.' (Arvind will make it to IIT.) And he did!

IIT was a whole new world. There was a library that was open from 8 a.m. to midnight. 'I can read as many books as I want here,' thought Arvind, who had not read much as a child. He would pore over the *Economic and Political Weekly* and started taking part in students' political rallies.

Illustrated by Priya Kuriyan

Arvind met students and lecturers who spoke endlessly about politics and the class divide, rights and development. 'Why can't we do something instead of just talking?' he thought. 'The children of the mess workers who serve us all day aren't even allowed to get admission in good schools.' He joined a group called Sahyog, which taught the children of the mess workers. With a friend's help, he even built a see-saw for them. Arvind went from door to door in the college hostel, asking, 'Will you donate just five rupees to help a poor child go to school?' Only a few did.

In 1975, Arvind joined the Tata Engineering and Locomotive Company (TELCO), now Tata Motors. A year in, he remembered Dr Anil Sadgopal, a guest lecturer at IIT, who taught science to children in rural Madhya Pradesh. He decided to take a year off and give that a try.

In the villages, there were no science labs. Every child was mugging things up without understanding what it meant. 'This is horrible!' Arvind thought. He went to the local 'haat' and bought some odds and ends – nuts, bolts, matchsticks, gears, rubber and metal strips – to design something that students could learn from. Soon the 'matchstick-cycle valve-tube Meccano' was ready. Arvind was thrilled. 'I can finally put my IIT education to good use,' he thought.

Later, he quit TELCO. Arvind's mother said, '*Theek kara naukri chhodi, ab kuch nek kaam karega.*' (It was the right thing to leave the job, now he will do something noble.) This gave Arvind the motivation he needed. In 1984, he moved to Pune, where he worked with a team of just three people. His vision was simple – to help the poorest of poor children learn science in a fun and magical way, using only scrap and trash.

He made 8,700 videos, which were uploaded on YouTube, and over the years ninety million teachers and students from all over the world have viewed them. A teacher from the Dominican Republic dubbed three hundred videos into Spanish. Educators and children in developing countries in Latin America have viewed them and used the lessons.

Teachers from Germany wrote to Arvind. They had used his lessons to teach the children of Syrian refugees too. They said hands-on learning was the best way to teach science to children.

Arvind ran a science club in a school in Pune for eight years. In his club was a young girl, Durga, who used to help her mother clean utensils in four houses every morning. Then, she would come to school. She loved science. Once, she made a simple turbine from a bottle. Her teachers were impressed. Durga worked diligently and stood second in her high school board exams.

The newspapers heard about her and wrote about this hardworking young girl. Soon cheques poured in with donations and Durga joined an engineering college, after which she landed a great job as an engineer. That's the impact Arvind's projects have had on students.

Speaking of the workshops he organises in municipal schools, Arvind says, 'When I see the gleam in a child's eye and a smile on their face, I know my job is done!'

PRASHANT BHUSHAN

IN THE PUBLIC INTEREST

Nineteen-year-old Prashant was often in the Allahabad court, watching his father argue on behalf of his clients. After completing his undergraduate studies, he thought, 'Let me study law, but informally keep studying both physics and philosophy – subjects that I love.'

In college, he found that most students would study only from guide-books. Prashant, on the other hand, always studied at least fifty per cent of the course – the parts he found most interesting. Once, during exams, someone shouted, 'What is this paper? Only two questions here are from the guidebook!' Suddenly, there was a chorus of loud voices, 'Walk out, walk out!' The students got up and left, but Prashant kept writing. Two students came to him and said, 'Come on, a walkout has been declared.' Prashant said, 'All right, then please walk out.' Irritated, the students grabbed his answer sheet and said, 'You will also have to come with us!' Prashant calmly replied, 'If you do this, there will be trouble.' In those days, Allahabad University was notorious for students carrying arms. The students thought Prashant had a weapon, so they left.

Prashant continued to write, but soon, the invigilator walked out too. An angry Prashant found him outside and went with him to the registrar's office. He told the registrar, 'Everyone has walked out, so I'll finish this exam in your office and submit it.' The registrar was baffled. 'Your submission is illegal now, because you have brought the paper outside the hall. Please leave!'

The students began to gossip. Who was this righteous lone ranger who insisted on taking the examination? His father was the law minister – had he got the questions in advance? He hadn't, of course.

Shortly afterwards, Prashant went to Princeton on a fellowship to study philosophy and physics. But he did not find the curriculum challenging. So he completed his master's degree and came back to India to work as a public interest lawyer.

Illustrated by Shruti Anand

Prashant fought a number of high-profile public-litigation cases over the years, many of them pro bono. He worked on several landmark cases – the Bhopal Gas Tragedy, the Narmada Bachao Andolan, the 2G corruption case. 'This is incredible,' he thought. 'For each case, I get to work with the finest experts in each area and learn so much!' Corrupt judges, politicians and corporate heads felt dread even at the mention of Prashant's name.

Having observed his crusade against corruption, Arvind Kejriwal asked Prashant to help him draft the Lokpal bill. Together, they formed the Aam Aadmi Party. But Prashant found Arvind's ways dictatorial and felt that he would use any means to win. Disillusioned, he left the party.

In 2017, Prashant heard a recording of a conversation between a middleman representing a medical college and a retired Orissa High Court judge. The college seemed to be bribing members of the judiciary to allow it to function, even though the Medical Council of India had declared the college sub-standard. In the recording, it seemed the judge was acting on behalf of the Chief Justice of India (CJI). Along with other lawyers, Prashant filed a petition in the Supreme Court asking for a special investigative team to monitor the case. But when a bench of judges was constituted, it included the CJI! An appalled Prashant told the CJI, 'It is not proper for you to hear this case, because it involves you directly.' He made his arguments in court and then walked out in protest.

Prashant started the Sambhaavnaa Institute of Public Policy and Politics – to shape and train young minds to fight for the public. 'We only live under an illusion that we have a functioning system of justice in this country,' he says ruefully. 'Actually, there isn't. And today we are probably worse off than ever! I, for my part, will continue to do whatever it takes to bring the judiciary back on track!'

Science-fiction buff that he is, he adds, 'Perhaps the only thing that can save us is superior artificial intelligence taking control of our planet.'

Illustrated by Udisha Madan

P. SAINATH

VOICE OF THE PEOPLE

Four-year-old Sainath was very close to his grandfather, V.V. Giri. He would often sit with Giri while he worked, keeping him company. Every now and then, the doting grandfather would give Sainath a sip of his steaming coffee. He would sip quietly, lest his grandmother caught him having coffee at such a young age – again!

One day, a Scottish gentleman came to meet Giri. He said, 'Do you remember me?' Giri didn't. The Scot handed Giri a piece of cloth. Giri laughed. 'Why on earth did you keep this?' he asked. The man said, 'I knew that some of you would make something of your lives.' That cloth was Giri's from when he was a prisoner during the British rule – it had his convict number. The Scotsman was a retired officer. Young Sainath didn't know any of this. As the Scot was leaving, he bent down to tell Sainath, 'I had your grandad in prison.' Sainath was most curious, and this was the beginning of his fascination with India's freedom struggle.

While studying for his master's in history at Jawaharlal Nehru University, Sainath began putting the freedom struggle into context. Gandhi, Nehru, Ambedkar, Sarojini Naidu – they all wrote. He thought, 'Journalism and the freedom struggle are more closely intertwined than I had imagined.'

So twenty-four-year-old Sainath joined United News of India, reporting to K.P.K. Kutty. 'I am training with the most precise copy editor ever,' he thought. When he moved to *The Daily* as foreign editor, its seventy-year-old editor R.K. Karanjia taught Sainath how to be a dexterous storyteller. RKK taught him the art of taking a simple, unknown person and putting them in the heart of a story that could even rock Parliament.

In the nineties, Sainath was sent to tour nine states that had been struck by drought. He felt lost. 'Where do I even start? No one has taught me how to report on tragedy and sorrow. How can I possibly ask people questions about their difficult times?' Instinctively, he started to walk with a family that had been dispossessed of their land by sahukars. They were walking from Vidarbha to Bombay and Sainath walked with them for a large part of their journey. When he came back, he wrote about it and won two prizes for his journalism. But Sainath didn't collect them. He felt his articles were not able to portray the power of what he had experienced. When he tracked the family down a year later, he was shocked. The women had entered the sex trade, the children were scavenging somewhere and the man was working as a porter.

Sainath told himself, 'I'll go back to the villages and do the stories the right way. I'll make sure the villagers are the front and centre of my stories. I'll provide a framework, and a lens for interpretation.' He applied for a fellowship and went back to rural India. He walked several kilometres every day, staying with farmers, miners, labourers and people from the fishing community all over the country. He felt it was the only way to get to the heart of a story. His articles became more insightful and nuanced than before. And he always refused to give people in power the last word.

Sainath took all the photographs that accompanied his stories. He spent so much time with the people he wrote about that they were hardly conscious of his camera and he managed to capture thousands of candid photos. Eventually, he wrote a book called *Everybody Loves a Good Drought*, which included all the essays from his reportage.

Once, Sainath did a story on the villages where major armed uprisings against the British had taken place. He went to each village to see how the people who had fought in those battles were faring. He thought, 'The current generation of Indians has never seen, heard or engaged with those everyday people who fought for their freedom. Let me document the stories of freedom fighters in the villages.' So, in 2022, he published *The Last Heroes: Foot Soldiers of Indian Freedom* with 16 powerful stories.

Sainath doesn't like to use the word 'poverty'. He prefers 'deprivation'. 'When you use the word poverty,' he says, 'it seems like a social disease and no one has any responsibility. "Deprivation" makes it clear that there is a depriver, someone who has actively deprived the under-privileged.'

SANJEEV JAIN

HEALING THE MIND

Sanjeev and his classmates from the Air Force Central School were marching at the annual Republic Day parade. Not in their school uniforms, but in Air Force blues! It was 1972, and the Indian forces were still at their forward posts, after having been deployed in the 1971 war. At the government's request, the school got some of its students to represent the soldiers. They spent a month in a freezing winter camp, training for the marchpast. By the end of it, Sanjeev was miserable. 'I just want to go home!' he thought.

Sanjeev had always loved science. When he graduated from school, he won a national science talent scholarship and enrolled in pre-medical studies at Delhi University (DU). Eventually, he joined Maulana Azad Medical College. College life was a mix of work, play and fun. There was an endless supply of LP records, and he and his mates would listen for hours to the Beatles, the Rolling Stones and lots of Hindi music, enjoy theatre performances at Mandi House, and visit the bookshops of Delhi. During the vacation, there was a course that focused on studying the brain. Sanjeev was hooked!

He considered specialising in surgery. But then he thought, 'Surgery is too intense for my liking. Psychiatry is so much more exciting. It's a culmination of chemistry, brain biology and the social conditions of a patient. That's what I want to study.'

During his training, Sanjeev worked with patients from all walks of life. A window-washer who wrote romantic poetry and sang loudly at night. A lawyer who came to believe the entire world was an illusion after a trip to an ashram, so much so that when his grandchild fell off the bed, he didn't pick him up, believing it to be an illusion. Some of the patients Sanjeev treated were surprisingly creative while undergoing manic episodes. He realised that treating mental illnesses required not only medication but also a deep understanding of people. Such illnesses were not restricted

Illustrated by Anisha Thampy

to one type of person, but were prevalent across regions and economic groups.

Then, for the first time, Sanjeev saw how people were addicted to drugs. For over a thousand years, Delhi had had a number of state-authorised afeem and bhang thekas (opium and hashish shops). Opium gave its users a sense of pleasant tranquillity, and many were addicted to it – from truck drivers to teachers. When Prime Minister Morarji Desai banned the sale of these drugs, there was chaos. Hundreds of people flocked to hospitals, but doctors had no idea how to treat withdrawal from opium-related drugs. A man lamented, 'All I need is a dana [a seed-size measure] a day. Why has the government taken away the little comfort I had?' Sanjeev realised then that even a small change in government policy can impact thousands of people.

Then Sanjeev moved to the National Institute of Mental Health and Neurosciences (NIMHANS) in Bangalore to study for an MD in psychiatry and joined the faculty soon after graduation. At the Biological Psychiatry Unit, he joined the team researching the brain, human genomes and molecules.

Sanjeev is a firm believer in the intersection of social studies and psychiatry. Once, he met a woman who suffered recurrent bouts of depression at a certain time of the year. It was a while before Sanjeev understood the underlying cause: the monsoon had caused the woman's hut to be washed away, around the same time, year after year. It made him realise even more acutely that while other streams of medicine had global tenets that everyone could follow, psychiatry was a deeply local health issue. How could anyone sitting in an urban First World setting understand the trauma of having their house washed away year after year?

Sanjeev was part of the committee tasked with drafting a mental-health policy document for India, and he continues to work with NGOs. He says, 'About seven per cent of the population suffers from mental illnesses. With the right treatment, most can live fairly independent, productive lives, but there are many with severe mental illnesses, who need prolonged treatment and support through life. But we have only 20,000 beds and more than five million ill people. The government must treat mental illness like any other and provide facilities for patients. Otherwise, people with serious illnesses will be left at the mercy of charity, which fluctuates and cannot be taken for granted.'

'One problem,' Sanjeev adds, 'is that mental health, even the profession of psychiatry, is still stigmatised. Even the plea of insanity is rarely used in India because of the shame attached to it. It is easier for us to say, "We are bad" rather than "we are mad".'

Sanjeev collaborates with teams of scientists across disciplines. They are working towards identifying and understanding genes specifically involved in brain functioning and diseases. This could help people who are at risk of developing mental illnesses.

Today, Sanjeev is considered one of India's leading experts in mental health research and public health policy. Ever reticent, he wears his considerable scholarship lightly.

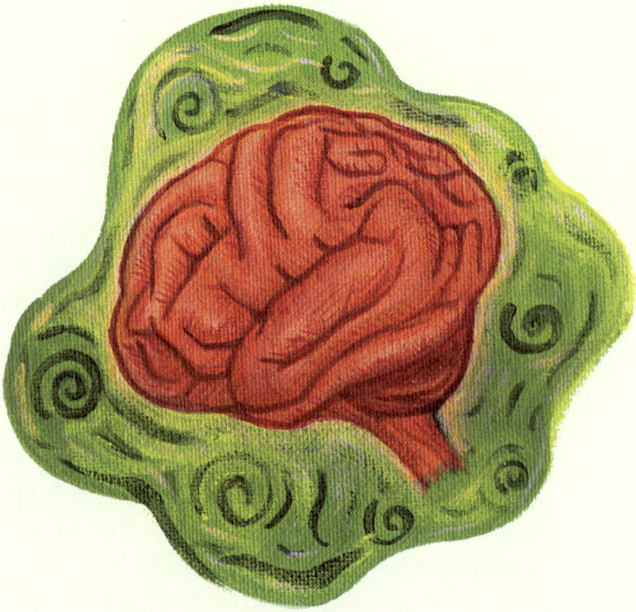

RAJENDRA SINGH

WATER MAN

Rajan's father was a landowner with vast fields and he employed Dalit workers. Rajan played with the children – running around and pulling up sweet carrots and radishes from the ground and munching on them together. His father wasn't pleased. '*Nalayak hain ye!*' They are worthless! Undeterred, Rajan shared his pencils and toys with his friends, and even his favourite treat – sweet and sticky homemade jaggery!

One day, Rajan announced, 'I want to be a farmer!' But his father was against it. 'Farming is not for you. I want you to study hard and join the government.'

Soon, young Rajan was off to Jaipur to study Ayurveda. After finishing his studies, he went to Alwar. Many of the village folk suffered from night blindness, and Rajan began treating them. One day, a man named Mangoo Lal Meena came to him and said, 'We don't want your medicine. We want water. Our land is dry and our crops are dead.' Rajan was perplexed. 'Mangoo kaka, I don't know how to help you. Ask the young men in the village to do it.' Mangoo Lal replied, 'They have all gone to the city to look for work. I will teach you how to get water.'

Rajan reluctantly agreed. He found himself being lowered into a dry well inside a leather sack. After five minutes, Mangoo Lal pulled him out. 'What did you see?' he asked. Rajan replied, '*Seedhi daraar.*' Straight lines. Mangoo said, 'You will find strong roots of trees where there are vertical gaps, and small bushes where there are horizontal gaps. That is how trees and plants look for water.'

The next day, Mangoo Lal came to Rajan with spades, shovels and axes. He led the young man to a dry area and said, 'Dig!' Then he gave instructions on how to build a crescent-shaped dam called a johad. Rajan used stones, mud and straw, and soon the johad was ready. 'Now when it

Illustrated by Akash Rajan

rains, the water will not run away from the hills. It will get collected here and will even recharge the groundwater,' said Mangoo Lal. Rajan thought, 'This is incredible. Yesterday, Mangoo Lal taught me hydro geomorphology, and today he has taught me civil engineering!'

Mangoo Lal said to Rajan, 'Stop treating people with medicine; treat the earth instead.' And so Rajan became an 'Earth Doctor'. In a couple of years, Mangoo Lal's village had abundant water, and the young men of the village began returning home from the city.

Rajendra then joined an organisation called Tarun Bharat Sangh and went with them to the village of Gopalpura. There, women walked almost one full day, just to get three pots of water for the family. Rajan would be given a small bowl, which could hold just a little more than half a litre of water. 'How will I bathe with this much?' he thought. Over the next few days, he learnt how to use a wet cloth efficiently, to clean himself in seventeen careful minutes.

The Arvari river in Gopalpura had been dry for decades. The Tarun Bharat Sangh built a johad at the source of the river. With the help of the villagers, they built over three hundred small mud dams along the dry riverbed. The groundwater started to get replenished, and one day, there was a miracle. The river started flowing again! Rajendra was ecstatic. People were now talking about his work and calling him the 'Water man of India'.

In 1986, after the work in Gopalpura was complete, Rajan felt the soil needed rejuvenation. He and the villagers planted trees. But the village collector didn't like what they were doing, so he fined Rajendra almost six thousand rupees! 'A fine for planting trees?' Rajendra was confused and wrote to people he knew to help him. The collector was reprimanded and transferred. Ever a pacifist, Rajan said to the villagers, 'The collector may be gone, but he will remain angry at our good work. Why don't we call him over to the village for a meal?' So the people of the village invited him and gifted him a statue of Lord Ganesh. They said, 'We hope Ganesh gives you some wisdom so that you behave better!' Needless to say, the collector walked off in a huff.

Rajendra and his team have built around 11,800 water reservoirs without any support from the government and have revived twelve water bodies. He fights against industry and mining which eat into the earth's water reserves.

Rajendra says, 'We are in the middle of a water crisis, and I wish children would make friends with nature.' His favourite piece of wisdom is from Gandhi: 'The earth can fulfil the needs of everyone, but cannot fulfil the greed of even one person.'

A. MURUGANANTHAM

PAD MAN

Murugan's mother was exhausted after a long day of labour. In her hand were five rupees – her daily wage. Even though she worked all day, she could not earn enough to support Murugan and his sisters or send them to school. Seeing her struggle, fourteen-year-old Murugan dropped out of school and took up welding and other odd jobs. He did this for the next decade.

In 1998, Murugan got married to Shanthi. One day, he saw his wife hiding something behind her back. 'What is that?' Murugan asked. 'None of your business,' she replied brusquely. Curious, Murugan ran after her and saw that Shanthi was holding some dirty rags. He realised then that she was using these for her period. When he asked her why, Shanthi said, 'If I buy pads from the market, it will cut into our milk money.'

Murugan was surprised to hear this. He immediately cycled to the nearest pharmacy and bought a packet of sanitary napkins. The chemist wrapped the packet in newspaper, which amused Murugan. Back home, he took apart a napkin and examined it carefully. 'This is just made of cotton,' he thought. 'Why do they cost so much? I am sure I can make these!'

Keen on impressing his wife with a more hygienic alternative than rags, Murugan began experimenting. When he finally created a design he thought would work, he asked Shanthi to try it. She replied that he would have to wait for a month: Murugan had no idea that periods occurred only once every month! And so, he waited. But when Shanthi finally used it, the verdict was disheartening. 'Terrible,' she said, 'I prefer my rags.' Undeterred, Murugan continued his experiments. He asked his sisters to test his next design. But they found it weird and refused to participate.

Murugan thought, 'I need more volunteers.' He approached a women's medical college and distributed the pads to students. He told them

Illustrated by Priyanka Paul

that the pads were free, but they would need to return the used ones to him. He would then sit for hours with the used pads to examine their absorbency. But before long, the women stopped taking part, worried that their blood was being used for black magic. At home, Shanthi did not like that Murugan was talking so freely about such a taboo topic, and she left him. Soon after, his mother walked out too. 'Murugan, I think you are under a witch's spell! It is making you collect all those pads with blood. I cannot stay here!' she said.

But Murugan did not give up. He bought a football bladder to use as a fake uterus and asked a butcher friend to give him goat's blood. Then he tied this fake uterus to himself and tested his handmade pads. He would walk in them, run in them and even cycle in them, pressing the bladder to see how the pads absorbed the blood. When people saw him washing his stained clothes at the village well, they thought that either he had a disease or spirits had possessed him. Murugan left the village before anyone could harm him. But, like a dedicated scientist, he did not give up on his research.

He wrote to some professors and learnt that pads were made of cellulose – an absorbent material made from plants. He got someone to send him two cellulose boards and experimented with them. Finally, after five years, he designed a machine made of wood that could manufacture low-cost pads. He took his invention to the Indian Institute of Technology, Madras. While the scientists were sceptical of this rudimentary wooden invention, they secretly entered the model in an innovation competition. To Murugan's delight, he bagged the first prize and was given an award by the President of India. By then, Shanthi and his mother had also returned home.

Spurred by this success, Murugan decided to supply his machines to rural areas in India where women had no access to sanitary napkins. But eventually, he made the design open source. Now, people all over the world can download the blueprint and customise the machine. And thus, Murugan has changed the lives of millions of women around the world.

There are three kinds of people, Murugan says: 'Uneducated, little educated and surplus educated.' Being a dropout, he considers himself 'little educated', but he is doing everything he can to change society for the better. He asks those who are 'surplus educated': 'What are you doing?'

JADAV PAYENG

GROWING TREES

Molai was distressed. Hundreds of snakes lay writhing and dying on the arid sandbar by the river Majuli. A few months earlier, the Brahmaputra had flooded due to the monsoon. Afterwards, the snakes had been left behind on the banks, along with the wreckage. They had taken shelter in the debris, but then, a drought hit. The land became dry and burning hot. There was no shade or trees where the snakes could hide.

Molai thought, 'Will we also die like this one day? What can I do to fix this?' The sixteen-year-old went to a village called Deuri, five kilometres away. There, he said to the elders, 'Please help me find a way to stop this tragedy.' The villagers gave him twenty-five saplings of bamboo and some seeds. 'Trees and plants will help. Sow these saplings,' they said. 'Bamboo is the tallest grass in the world, and it can survive in harsh weather.'

Molai went back to the dry riverbank. Using a long wooden stick, he dug a hole and planted a sapling. Every day, he would cross the river to plant another. He did this for many years. When it rained, the bamboo flourished and more grew. During dry spells, they would turn brown, but they didn't die. The banks of the Brahmaputra were now lush with so many bamboo trees that insects started coming to Molai's little patch of green.

Then something incredible happened. The soil began to change and became fertile. Molai, or Jadav as he was known, was excited. 'Now, I can plant other kinds of trees too,' he thought. The first one he planted was a teak. Then he planted some more – silk cotton, lebek and different varieties of grass. 'If I plant my saplings and seeds just before the monsoon, they can benefit from the rains. The rest of the year, I can collect seeds from the forest,' he thought. For twenty-five years, Jadav patiently tended the land.

Illustrated by Ayesha Broacha

One day, he heard chirping. He looked up and saw birds among the trees; his patch was now a jungle. Slowly the deer followed, and then came the gibbons, buffaloes, elephants and even tigers. Jadav owned a few cows and sold milk for a living. When the tigers came, they killed a couple of cows. But he didn't mind. 'It's their food, and this is the cycle of life.'

But now, there was another problem – poachers! They came stealthily to kill the animals and cut down his beloved trees.

One day, a wildlife photographer, Jitu Kalita, was exploring the Brahmaputra. When he looked at the horizon, he saw a forest in the distance. 'How can this be?' he thought. Jitu went closer and couldn't believe his eyes. Here was a dense, lush jungle in the middle of a sandy wasteland. He saw a man and followed him. It was Jadav. But when Jadav saw Jitu, he mistook him for a poacher and jumped up to fight! It took Jitu a long while to convince Jadav that he was a harmless photographer. When he finally calmed down, Jitu asked, 'But who are you?' Jadav told him about how he had been planting saplings since 1979 to create this forest – all 550 hectares of it.

Jitu was so impressed, he wrote an article in a newspaper about Jadav's incredible achievement. Finally, the world got to know about him. Former President Abdul Kalam presented Jadav with an award and gave him the title of the 'Forest Man of India'.

Jadav talks to his trees just like he talks to his family. He especially loves talking to the first teak tree he planted, which is now large and green. 'If it weren't for you, no one would know about us and this amazing forest. People from all over the world come here to meet us.'

The forest is now called Molai after Jadav. He says, 'All of us are animals; some of us just wear clothes. Yet, the biggest threat to the environment and the animals is humankind!' Jadav believes that if every child is responsible for one tree, then in ten years, India will be green!

Illustrated by Tara Anand

BEZWADA WILSON

DIGNITY FIRST

Bezwada was leaving his school in the Kolar Gold Fields, when some boys walked up to him. 'Your school is so small!' they mocked. Bezwada retorted, 'But we have the biggest tree!' 'But you don't have benches to sit on!' they continued. 'We have the freedom to sit anywhere!' Bezwada shot back. The other kids were now angry. They sneered, 'You are a bhangi, you are a bhangi's son!' Bezwada was stumped! 'Does being a bhangi make me bad?' he thought, as he walked home dejectedly.

Bezwada's mother insisted her son get a good education. So, after a few years of studying in his neighbourhood school, he moved to a bigger school. In the first few weeks, the teachers would ask, 'What do your parents do?' Bezwada's family belonged to a community of Dalits. The caste system dictated that Dalits were responsible for manual scavenging – cleaning latrines and carrying the excreta of the upper castes. Bezwada would just keep his head down and sit silently. He decided that he would skip the first month of school every year so he didn't have to answer this question.

When he was a little older, Bezwada's brother said, 'We need money in the family. Bezwada, come, let's get you enrolled at the employment exchange.' But the officer said, 'Your surname is Wilson. I don't care how educated you are, there is only one kind of job you people can do!' Bezwada was outraged. He tore up the form and walked out.

Bezwada noticed that people in his community used to come home completely drunk and beat their wives in frustration. 'Please do not drink, it is not good,' he would request the men. They said, 'If we do not drink, we will not be able to do the job we do. You think it's easy? Come with us and see what we do every day.'

One day, Bezwada went with the others to a community toilet. It was an open space. People would go there to defecate and then leave without cleaning up. A person from Bezwada's community would collect the excreta in a bucket and take it to a pit. Later, they would collect the waste from the pit, load it on a tractor and unload it on the outskirts of the village.

As they worked, Bezwada saw a man's bucket slip out of his hands into a pit of excreta. The man rolled up his sleeves and put his hand into the sludge, rummaging for his bucket. Bezwada was aghast. 'Please, please, this is not right. How can you do this?' he asked. The man said, 'This is my job, my life. Our community has been doing this for more than a century.' 'This is inhuman!' Bezwada yelled 'We cannot do this. It's better for us to die without food than do a job like this!' But everyone ignored him. His brother took him by the arm. 'Bezwada, you're right. But no one listens to us.'

Bezwada decided to channel his anger on behalf of every manual scavenger. He took photos of the work, wrote letters threatening the mining authorities, and even wrote to the prime minister and the chief minister. The media picked up the story, and finally, the mining company demolished the toilets. The hundred-odd manual scavenging workers there were reallocated to other jobs. This was Bezwada's first victory.

He soon began his activism in other states, and after multiple campaigns, the Government of India passed the Employment of Manual Scavengers and Construction of Dry Latrines (Prohibition) Act in 1993. But Bezwada was still angry. While the district collector could take action against people for not following this law, not a single one actually did so. Even the Indian Railways continued to illegally employ people to pick up excreta from the rail tracks.

When Bezwada learnt about Ambedkar and his vision of equality, he started the 'Safai Karamchari Andolan'. The goal of this movement is to eliminate manual scavenging in India. Every day, he continues to fight for the rights of people still working in manual scavenging.

Bezwada says, 'What is the point of building latrines when you still make women from our community pick up your excreta? Men are lowered into street sewers to unclog them. Some die. But no one does anything! When you tell someone, "You are a bhangi" you should be ashamed of yourself,' says Bezwada. 'You are *creating* the shit. We are *cleaning* it. You are the one who is dirty.'

'I don't need your tears or your sympathy,' he declares. 'I need your anger – to change this system in our country!'

PERUMAL MURUGAN

ALIVE AND UNAFRAID

There was a drought in the village of Tiruchengode. Murugan and his brother had just come back from school and were following a man holding a coconut suspended from a string. When the coconut started to move in a circular arc, the man yelled, 'Dig here, there is water underneath!' Murugan, along with other villagers, started to dig. They dug deep until they finally hit water. Overjoyed, everyone rushed to fill up their buckets.

Murugan's father owned a piece of farmland and also ran a soda shop near a cinema theatre. Sometimes, Murugan helped out at the shop. He would watch the customers closely. 'Why do they speak to the children who work in the shop so rudely?' he thought. It was a while before he realised that this prejudice was on account of their caste.

Murugan's father wanted him to be a professor. While in college, Murugan loved to read and even wrote lyrics for All India Radio, Trichy. After completing his Ph.D. in Tamil literature, he started teaching. On the side, he would write little stories. But soon, he thought, 'This is not enough. I want to write about life – about caste, about real issues, about my people!' So Murugan wrote a longer story, about how the housing board took away their land in the village and the misery they went through. When this novel, *Eru Veyyil*, was published, Murugan shot to fame.

Murugan met and married a fellow Tamil professor. But she belonged to a different caste. When Murugan's mother found out, she was so ashamed, she refused to leave her house for months. He was shocked that his own mother was casteist!

Murugan's mother was worried about where she would be buried after her death. 'You married someone from a different caste. What if they do not bury me in this village ground because of you?' So Murugan paid temple tax in three different villages, just in case the burial was refused in one. But when his mother died in 2012, he turned away from the idea of caste altogether and chose the electric crematorium for her.

Illustrated by Sadhna Prasad

Meanwhile, Murugan continued to write stories of his village. One day, his wife said, 'Murugan, how many more stories will you write about this place? There really can't be any more stories to tell!' But Murugan always found another. He had a wicked sense of humour. He named one of his books *Pee Kadaigal* (Shit Tales)! It included a story of a man who jumps into a septic tank. The title shocked readers, and many were too embarrassed to buy it.

The end of 2014 was heartbreaking for Murugan and his family. Local leaders said that Murugan's novel *Mathorubagan* was offensive to the community, especially to women. A bandh took place in Namakkal, Murugan's hometown, and he and his family were threatened. The police tried to mediate a discussion between him and the protestors. Murugan said, 'I will remove all references to the place where events in the novel take place.' But the protestors wanted more. Murugan thought, 'If my writing is causing distress, I wonder if I should even be doing it.' He withdrew his book.

In January 2015, Murugan's fans woke up to an alarming Facebook post: 'Author Perumal Murugan is dead. He is no God. Hence, he will not resurrect. Hereafter, only P. Murugan, a teacher, will live.' He requested his publishers to recall his books from the market and asked his readers to burn his books. Then, Murugan and his wife abandoned their home of seventeen years and moved to Chennai. Murugan felt like a refugee, trapped in their apartment in the city. Even though he met 300 students a day at the college where he taught, his mind shut down. 'I just can't bring myself to read a book, write or attend literary meetings. I feel like a dead man walking,' he said.

Eventually, the People's Union for Civil Liberties filed a petition in the Madras High Court, alleging that the police had coerced Murugan to withdraw from writing. The court agreed and made a beautiful argument for why his books should be published and read. The judges declared, 'Let the author be resurrected to do what he is best at. Write.' Murugan thought, 'The last line of the judgement is an order for me. I have to respect it.' And to the delight of his readers, he began writing again. His book Poonachi: The Story of a Goat became popular the world over. In 2023, his novel Pyre was long-listed for the International Booker Prize.

When asked about the one thing he wants to change most, Murugan says, 'I want to destroy caste in this country!'

Illustrated by Aparajitha Vaasudev

SONAM WANGCHUK

CHANGING LIVES

There was no school in Sonam's village, so his mother home-schooled him till he was eight and a half years old. She sang to him and read him stories. Sonam's uncle took him from village to village. 'Read this signboard on the shop, Sonam,' he would say. Often, he would turn on the radio and ask Sonam questions about the programme.

One day, his uncle said, 'It's time for you to go to school.' Sonam was sent to a school near the border. Shortly after, his father was posted to Srinagar. Sonam got admission in a Kendriya Vidyalaya, but he hated it there. His classmates constantly teased him. 'I've come first,' a boy boasted in his class. 'So what?' Sonam shot back. 'I've come thirty-first!' He thought a higher number meant a better rank.

Learning in English and Urdu was tough for Sonam – he couldn't speak either. One day, overcome with frustration, Sonam ran away to Delhi where he pleaded with teachers at the Vishesh Kendriya Vidyalaya to enrol him. They agreed, and Sonam moved there. He got better at communication and learnt to debate. He even took to theatre.

Sonam loved science and was obsessed with concave mirrors. 'I wonder if I can use these as lights for dark areas. Can we use them for cooking?' He had so many questions! One of his uncles said to him, 'Why don't you study mechanical engineering? You'll get all your answers!' But his father said, 'What good is mechanical engineering? You should do civil engineering. If you don't, I won't support you!'

Sonam was adamant and enrolled in mechanical engineering at a college in Srinagar. 'How will I pay three hundred rupees every month?' he wondered. And then he had an idea. There was a boom in tuition centres for children in Ladakh, but they charged huge fees. So, during the winter break, Sonam rented a large space, hired a secretary and bought a cyclostyling machine. He began teaching students at one-fifth the cost of a tuition centre. All this when he barely had money for lunch!

He thought, 'Let me spend extra time with the smarter kids. They can then teach the weaker kids. When the weaker kids learn and get smarter, they can teach the next lot of weaker kids. It's a self-sustaining cycle.' And that's what he did. Slowly, not only did Sonam earn enough to pay his college fees, but he also helped kids improve in their studies.

After he finished college, Sonam thought, 'Why are ninety-five per cent of the children failing in schools in Ladakh? It's not because they are not smart. Something is not working.' So he started a school that admitted students with one unique qualification: 'failed in class ten'. Sonam didn't believe the children were failures; he believed that the system had failed them.

He noticed that in winter, when the children came to school, they could barely move. 'The temperature outside is –25°C, and inside it is –10°C. Children are freezing. How can I expect them to learn?' he thought. Investing in solar energy and using special insulation techniques in his mud school, Sonam ensured that the temperature was at least 14°C. Now, the children could study comfortably.

Sonam wanted to improve the facilities even more. 'We face a huge water shortage in April and May. But after that, when the glaciers melt, we get billions of litres of water, which go waste!' He knew that if ice was frozen in large sheets on the ground, it would melt easily in the sun. 'We can't possibly provide shade to the ice,' he thought. One day, he had a brainwave. 'What if we channel running water to build narrow conical ice mountains with very small surface areas?'

He gathered volunteers and students from his school, and together they built these in the upper valley of Phyang. They called them Ice Stupas. Now, the ice would melt slowly. The water would trickle down to the lower inhabited areas, where people could use it for farming in the dry months. The model was so successful that graduating students piloted the Ice Stupa Project in other countries like Switzerland and Peru.

'Success doesn't come from privilege alone. Even difficulties can become opportunities and can be turned to your advantage,' Sonam says.

Illustrated by Sudeepti Tucker

A.R. RAHMAN

BEYOND BOUNDARIES

A sophisticated new piece of equipment was in the house. 'What is this, appa?' five-year-old Rahman asked. 'It's a Japanese synthesiser – the first one in South India,' Shekhar said proudly. 'Come, I will teach you.' Rahman loved practising with his father, a popular and respected musician in the Malayalam film industry.

When Rahman was nine, his father passed away from cancer. His mother had to rent Shekhar's instruments to musicians and studios to make money. 'Why don't you learn to play the keyboard?' she told her son. One of Shekhar's friends, a music composer for Malayalam films, gave young Rahman work at his recording sessions. Eleven-year-old Rahman's talent was evident, and word got around about the boy and his magic fingers. Multiple film studios hired him as a keyboard player. He started experimenting with electronic equipment and midi players and also composed jingles for ad films. When juggling work and school became difficult, he decided to focus full time on his music career.

Around this time, an ad agency was looking for someone to do the music for a film against drug abuse. They heard about the nineteen-year-old composer and decided to try him. On the designated morning, they waited for Rahman to arrive. But they kept waiting. Rahman used to compose until late in the night and could never wake up on time.

After many hours, a number of massive boxes were brought into the studio. Finally, Rahman walked in and smiled. The people from the agency were outraged. 'Who does he think he is? Walking in late and then not even apologising!' Swallowing their anger, they told Rahman what the ad was about. He listened quietly and said, 'Okay, come back in an hour.' When they came back an hour later, they were blown away. 'This sounds so professional! We don't have to change a thing.' Rahman turned to them and said, 'Is it okay? It's just a basic tune; I will do more work on it.'

People from the ad agency were impressed and started working with Rahman, who went on to compose more than 300 jingles. They also told film director Mani Ratnam about him. One day, Mani visited Rahman's studio to listen to his music. After a while, he stood up, thanked Rahman and walked out. Rahman was confused. He turned to his friend Trilok, who had introduced them. '*Enna da? Onnumae sollalai.*' (What man? He didn't say anything!) A few days later, Mani called Rahman. 'I am signing you on as the music director for my next film, *Roja*.'

Rahman was born Dilip, but he didn't think the name 'fit' him. He wanted to change it and build a new identity. His mother, who had long since embraced Sufism, had a dream that the name should start with Ar. They went to a Hindu astrologer, who said he should change his name to Abdul Rahman, and his mother finally decided on Allahrakha Rahman. Rahman loved the sound of his new name. His mother told Mani Ratnam, 'Can you change Dilip's name in the film credits to A.R. Rahman?' Ratnam did. Rahman was reading a book called *The 99 Names of Allah*, and in it he saw that the first name was Ar Rahman. 'This is a sign,' he thought. 'I have to respect and elevate this name.'

Roja and its music were a resounding success, and Rahman and Mani went on to collaborate again. Rahman became one of the most sought-after music directors. He was soon composing for Bollywood – even though he didn't understand a word of Hindi! A few years later, he was off to London to work with Andrew Lloyd Webber. When *Bombay Dreams* debuted, the crew got a standing ovation of thirteen minutes twenty seconds. A nervous Rahman was even introduced to the Queen of England.

Once, during Ramzan, Rahman woke up to record a song. His sound engineers were missing, so he called Bharat Bala, with whom he was working on an album. In the recording room, Rahman passionately belted out a few verses of a song he had composed, 'Maa Tujhe Salaam'. When he came out, Bala was crying. 'What happened? Did I do something wrong?' Rahman asked. Bala replied, 'No, it was fantastic!' The song was released in 1997, on Independence Day.

Rahman has since gone on to perform internationally. He famously composed the music for the movie *Slumdog Millionaire* and won two Oscars for it.

Rahman says, 'Everything teaches you something! If my father hadn't suffered, I wouldn't have melancholy in my music. If I didn't fast during Ramzan, I wouldn't be able to feel the hunger of the poor man.'

I.M. VIJAYAN

MAGIC IN HIS FEET

Ten-year-old Vijayan was at the Thrissur Municipal Corporation Stadium with a box of objects hung around his neck. 'Sodaaaa, peeeanuts, beeeeedi, cigarette ...' he yelled into the crowd, stealing a glance at the football match that was being played. For every bottle of soda he sold, he earned ten paise. At the end of the day he sat and counted his money. 'Eighteen ... nineteen ... twenty rupees!' He ran home to his parents. They lived in a Dalit colony close to the stadium.

Vijayan loved to play football. He would play on the streets or in the stadium itself, where he took his buffalo to graze on the green grass. He would collect deflated balls he found on the streets and kick them through a tall metal structure with three rings. Never good at studies, Vijayan failed five times in class five. 'I wish I could just play football all day! My friends are now in grade ten. Everyone calls me "chetta" (older brother) in my class!'

One day, Jose, a local coach, told Vijayan, 'Join my Sharjah Club; I will coach you.' Vijayan's father loved football too, and he encouraged his son. They couldn't afford to buy a ball, so he used cloth tied together – a 'thunipanthu' – and played barefoot.

When Jose saw a Sports Council advertisement inviting talented Thrissur football players to join, he asked Vijayan to try out. The skinny twelve-year-old went up against 150 other boys. The committee saw how intuitively Vijayan played and selected him. At the camp, Vijayan was in awe of the facilities. 'Three meals a day with fresh eggs, milk and bananas? Special shoes for football? This is a dream!' He trained so hard that the coach took him aside and said, 'Slow down, you are still very thin. Build your stamina and get strong first!' Vijayan trained there for three years.

Once camp ended, Vijayan lost focus for a while. His father had died, and his mother was struggling to make ends meet. They struggled even for basic resources like electricity. Still, she encouraged Vijayan to play. Vijayan thought, 'Let me play in the Sevens. At least I can make some money.' Sevens was a local version of football popular in Kerala, with only seven players in a team. Huge betting crowds supported it. Vijayan earned thirty to forty rupees per match and gave it all to his mother.

Once, there was a trial for the Kerala Police team, and the Director General of Police spotted him. 'This young man plays brilliantly! But he is only seventeen and not eligible to join the police yet. Let me convince him to stay here and use him as an extra until he turns eighteen!' Vijayan happily joined the Kerala Police and began playing with them. He was the youngest player and the only one to have trained in football. Everyone liked this cheerful boy. During a match in Delhi, Vijayan did a side flip and scored a goal. The crowd rose up to cheer. A senior police officer was watching the match. He came up to Vijayan and said, 'That was absolutely brilliant, Vijayan. You are a star!' And he handed him five hundred rupees. After that match, people began noticing the talented young man.

A few years later, much to the anger of his fans, Vijayan signed with the Mohun Bagan Athletic Club. Vijayan was unmoved. 'I am getting more money there, and it is important for me to support my family,' he said. In Calcutta, he soon had new fans. They called him 'Kalo Hiren'. 'What does that mean?' he asked. He was told it meant black deer – that when he dribbled the ball, his movements were as graceful as a deer's.

Vijayan played for six different football clubs over the years. In 1989, he played for the Indian national team. He had a knack for scoring goals from any position in the field. In a match against Bhutan, he scored a goal that had the crowd cheering. His coach Sukhwinder told him, 'Vijayan, you have scored the fastest goal in football – in twelve seconds.' Vijayan didn't quite understand the significance of this and was so focused on the game that he just said, 'Fine, sir!'

Vijayan went on to captain the Indian team and scored forty goals for the country. He formed an impressive striking partnership on the field with Sikkim's Bhaichung Bhutia. Within India, he scored two hundred goals – the highest number yet by an individual in the domestic sport. Now retired and over fifty years old, Vijayan still coaches and plays football. One can find him in the stadiums in Kochi, kicking footballs around in the late evenings.

INDIA

Illustrated by Aparajita Ninan

BHAICHUNG BHUTIA

SIKKIMESE SNIPER

'Great catch! Great catch!' yelled Bhaichung's dorm-in-charge, Leonard Lefvere. They were in the audio-visual room of the Tashi Namgyal Academy in Gangtok, watching a cricket match between Zimbabwe and New Zealand. The fielder, Martin Crowe, had just taken a tough catch.

Bhaichung said in a small voice, 'Sir, what's so great about that catch?' Leonard showed Bhaichung the replays, explaining why it had been a difficult one. 'No, it wasn't!' Bhaichung insisted. 'I can do it.' Leonard responded, 'Bhaichung, you play football here. You don't know much about cricket. You won't be able to catch a ball this way – running backwards!' But Bhaichung refused to accept that, and to the enjoyment of his housemates, a challenge was set.

Early the next morning, Leonard went to the field. Ten-year-old Bhaichung and his friends were already waiting. Leonard explained the method. 'You have to run backwards while keeping your eyes on the ball and then catch it.' Leonard hit the ball – high above Bhaichung's head. Bhaichung ran without taking his eyes off it and caught the ball. 'That's a fluke,' Leonard said, hitting the ball again – this time farther away. Bhaichung ran and flung himself lengthwise and still managed to catch the ball neatly. Thrilled with himself, he did a couple of cartwheels, delighting his friends no end. Lenny sir had lost the challenge!

Once, Leonard went to visit Bhaichung while he was ill with jaundice and kept in isolation. There, he saw Bhaichung jumping around the room, kicking a football. He could never sit still.

By the time he was ready for his tenth-grade examinations, Bhaichung had already played football at the biggest inter-school tournament – the Subroto Cup – and won the 'Best Player' award. Two months before the exam, he received a letter. He had been selected for the Under-Sixteen national team camp! 'This is a dream come true,' he thought excitedly. 'But how will I convince my parents to let me leave school and attend the camp?' He somehow mustered up the courage, but as he had expected, they refused. He tried again. 'I won't be able to focus on my studies, so I won't do well in any case. Please let me go.' They weren't happy, but they agreed. The camp was to be held in Kerala, and his mother dropped him off at the Gangtok railway station. The fifteen-year-old was off – alone on a long train journey that would take three days and nights.

When Bhaichung returned, he re-enlisted in school and sat for his exams. Just as he was finishing up, he got a call. 'You have been selected to join the East Bengal Football Club.' Bhaichung was ecstatic! He was now going to play with some of the best football players in the country.

In the course of his career, Bhaichung transferred from club to club, switching positions from midfield to striker, adroitly scoring goal after goal, winning accolades – the 'Golden Boot', 'Top Scorer', 'Indian Player of the Year' and 'Outstanding Player'. He even played with his childhood hero I.M. Vijayan, who declared Bhaichung 'God's gift to football'!

At the age of twenty-two, Bhaichung captained the Indian football team. Soon, he was offered a professional contract by the Bury Football Club in England. There he learnt both professionalism and even more humility because while he was a star back in India, no one had even heard of him in England!

In 2008, Bhaichung was chosen to carry the Olympic torch from India to Beijing, but he wrote to the Olympic Committee and refused. 'I am a Buddhist. I have many Tibetan friends in Sikkim. With this act, I want to show my solidarity to the people of Tibet and their struggle.' He was among many around the world who distanced themselves from the games, condemning China's stance on Tibet.

Bhaichung retired from football in 2011. 'I've enjoyed every moment of it,' he said. 'I would want to be remembered as just a footballer.'

He is ambitious for Indian football. 'It's important that the biggest names in sports speak out and demand better facilities, better training, better infrastructure. And that is how the sport will grow,' he says.

Illustrated by Hanisha Tirumalasetty

VISHWANATHAN ANAND

WORLD CHAMPION

'Amma, teach me how to play chess,' said six-year-old Anand to his mother. His mother was an excellent chess player. Anand was fascinated with the game and would wait eagerly for every issue of the chess magazine *64* to come home. 'Come on, Anand, lunch is served,' his parents would call. But there was no getting Anand to the dining table until he had read the magazine from cover to cover.

When he was nine years old, Anand's family moved to the Philippines for a few years. His mother was soon addicted to a daytime television show, where a host would analyse the latest chess matches, move by move. At the end of the show, there was a puzzle. If you solved it, you could win a book on chess – and these were rare then. Anand's mother would make notes and when Anand returned from school, she would say, 'Anand, sit with me. I'll teach you what was on TV today.' She would take him through the game and then give him the puzzle. 'A chess book as a prize? I need to win this!' Anand started sending in answers and he won each time! After he had won six books, the organisers of the show invited him over. 'Anand, this is our studio chess library. Choose as many books as you want; just stop sending us entries. You always win!' they told him. Anand chose some books, which he may never have found otherwise.

When they moved back to Madras, the chess scene was buzzing. At chess clubs, whoever lost had to go to the back of the line and wait to play again. 'I hate waiting, so I need to keep winning,' Anand thought. He loved blitz – a variation in chess in which each player had only ten minutes to complete the game. He became known as the 'Lightning Kid'. He began playing matches at the state and national levels, and at sixteen, he became the national champion! People started calling him the 'Tiger from Madras'.

Like sledging in cricket, chess players use psychological techniques to distract their opponents. In one of his games, Anand's opponent spun his keychain on his finger constantly. 'This is hugely distracting,' thought Anand. 'What can I do?' For the rest of the match, Anand wore a cap that shaded his eyes. Now, he could only see the board and not his annoying opponent.

Anand went on to become World Junior Chess Champion. 'I need to practise a lot more and play against better players,' he thought. He backpacked all over Europe with his handy sleeping bag in tow. But it was not easy. Money was running out. Once, he and six other chess players had to share a hotel room meant for two people. Every time a member of the staff came into the room, four of them would hide in the bathroom. All that struggle paid off, and at eighteen, Anand became India's first grandmaster!

In 1995, Anand played for the World Championship against the legendary grandmaster Garry Kasparov at the World Trade Center in New York. Anand won a few games, but then Garry started his psychological tricks to get to him. He would make a quick move and slam the door loudly on his way out to the players' lounge. It was intimidating, but Anand didn't complain. In the end, Vishy – as he was now called – lost the match, and Garry retained his title.

Anand went on to win the title of world champion six times. He was the only player to play the championships in various formats – tournament, match, knockout and rapid time controls – and win in all.

Anand believes it is important for children to start playing chess young. He says, 'Nowadays, using a computer, one can achieve the same level of preparedness as a grandmaster. There is no longer a difference between someone born in Moscow and on a Pacific island.'

About eighteen months after Anand became a grandmaster, he was travelling by train. A man sitting near him struck up a conversation. 'What do you do?' he asked. Anand replied, 'I am a chess player.' The man said, 'Okay, but what do you really do?' Anand said, 'No, I really am a chess player. I play quite seriously.' The man replied, 'Young man, let me give you some advice. Sport is risky. I mean, if you were Vishwanathan Anand, you could do it. But in your case, it seems like a hazard.' Anand smiled but didn't tell the man that he was Vishwanathan Anand. He says, 'It was one of the greatest moments of my life!'

PULELLA GOPICHAND

MASTER COACH

Gopi was showing off to the older neighbourhood kids that he could cross the street with his eyes closed. 'Do it again, Gopi, and we will give you a toffee!' the children egged him on. One day, in the middle of his 'performance', a cyclist hit Gopi – the brake lever dangerously close to striking his eye. The commotion brought his mother running. She found Gopi fighting with the cyclist. 'I'll take you to the police station,' threatened five-year-old Gopi. This, when he was in the wrong!

When Gopi and his family moved to Hyderabad, Gopi's father took his sons to join badminton coaching at the Fateh Maidan. Coach Hamid Hussain noticed the hardworking youngster and took him on. He soon became Hamid's favourite. Once, on tour, Gopi asked Hamid to teach him how to jump-smash. 'Please!' he begged. But Hamid refused. 'Gopi, your legs are not long enough.' A senior coach, Mohammed Arif, noticed the sulking twelve-year-old, who was constantly trying to do better. Arif would eventually become Gopi's coach and mentor.

At school, Gopi was often late or didn't submit his homework. His annoyed teachers made him stand outside the class. One day, there was an announcement over the loudspeaker. 'Congratulations to Gopichand for winning the state badminton match and making the school proud.' All the students burst into applause, and Gopi grinned, continuing to stand where he was, in the middle of his punishment!

On the court, however, Gopi moved from strength to strength, winning titles for the state. He started taking part in national competitions. After Coach Arif sent Gopi for a national training camp under a Chinese coach, his technique improved dramatically. Soon, he was playing in international matches. 'I am beating big players, but why am I not winning a final?' Gopi wondered. A few years later, he found out that he had sinusitis, which would get aggravated under a fan and in coastal cities. Now,

Illustrated by Maha Satish

whenever Gopi played in a coastal city like Goa, he wore a sweater, no matter how hot it was. When he finished playing, he would go straight to his dorm and sleep – without a fan.

Gopi trained at Prakash Padukone's academy where his game became well-rounded. People thought he was one of the most dedicated and aggressive young players. During a match, Gopi suffered a painful ligament tear, which required two surgeries. 'I hope I can play again,' he said worriedly to his doctor. 'Don't worry,' the doctor replied. 'Your knee is now stronger than before.' So Gopi got back to playing.

In 2000, he entered the Olympics, but the cemented courts took a toll on his knee again. Gopi lost the match. He had desperately wanted to win a medal for India. He was heartbroken, yet he continued to dream of winning. He had to talk himself back to reality. 'Boss, it's not happening. *Olympics toh khatam ho gaya hai.*' (The Olympics are done.)

But all was not lost. Gopi took part in the All England Championships in 2001. There, he shared a room with another player. As always, Gopi wouldn't turn the fan on. Once, his roommate woke in the middle of the night to a scary noise, only to find Gopi doing his pranayama! When they were installing a TV in the room, Gopi said, 'I don't want one. It will break my concentration!' This was the final straw – Gopi's roommate was furious and moved out! But Gopi's vision was clear; he had to beat the Chinese and Indonesian players.

Gopi played his way through each match and reached the finals, to play against the formidable Chen Hong. The match was tough, but Gopi's hard work paid off. He went on to become only the second man from India to win the All England Cup. The first was Prakash Padukone.

Gopi came home to a magnificent reception and many endorsement deals. He told his manager he would never endorse unhealthy products, no matter how much money was offered – no cigarettes, no alcohol, no aerated drinks.

In 2003, Gopi retired from active sport. He set up a state-of-the-art academy – the Pullela Gopichand Badminton Academy. It had every facility that Gopi never had the use of in his years of training. He now coaches many champions – P.V. Sindhu, Saina Nehwal, Srikanth Kidambi,

Parupalli Kashyap. He expects all his players to have the same dedication, aggression and focus he had. He gives his students the same priceless advice a Chinese coach had given him after he lost the Dutch Open: 'It is not how many times you fall or how hard you fall, it is each time you get up that counts.'

JOSY JOSEPH

DAVID AND GOLIATH

Eight-year-old Josy was on his way to church, walking across the paddy fields with his cousins, when they saw a dangerous-looking dog approach them. 'Don't run, stay calm,' Josy said, but his cousins didn't listen. Amidst the confusion, the dog bit Josy. When he went for the painful anti-rabies injections he thought, 'I deserve this. I am a sinner, I am paying for the sins of my forefathers and this is how I get punished.' The Catholic rhetoric was deeply ingrained in him.

After college, Josy moved to Delhi, keen on joining the civil services. But fate pushed him to the newsroom, where his editor told him to write a story on Rajan Pillai – the biscuit baron. He started his story: 'Rajan Pillai, who looks like a Latin-American middleweight boxer ...' The profile was greatly appreciated, and Josy was sucked into journalism. He decided to enrol in an evening journalism course at the YMCA Institute for Media Studies and Information Technology.

Once, after a long day at work, Josy was late for class. The teacher was handing out answer sheets from a mid-term exam. He asked Josy, 'Who are you? I have never seen you in my class.' Josy explained that he was late because of his job, but the teacher ignored him. Later, he confided to Josy, 'Yours was the best answer sheet I have checked in years.' Josy's practical training had held him in good stead.

For the first few years, Josy worked as a desk editor. Then he was sent to attend a press conference. The conference was in Punjabi and Josy couldn't understand a word. He came back and told his editor, 'I can't be a reporter. I can't speak these languages.' The editor said, 'Nonsense, language isn't the most important skill for a journalist. Fairness and a sense of curiosity are. You can hire an interpreter!'

Josy grew up with a deep sense of insecurity, so he would always recheck his facts and sources. He only filed stories after thoroughly vetting them. Over the years, he built his sources and would not trust the 'leaked documents' handed to him, because those could have some ulterior

Illustrated by Priya Kuriyan

purpose or could even be forged. At that time, there were very few investigative journalists, and twenty-two-year-old Josy quickly made a name for himself. 'This boy is not coming to me just for a sound byte,' people in power realised. 'He can bite back.'

Josy broke stories that exposed not only political corruption but also corporate–government nexuses and scams. The first time he was offered a bribe – an apartment – he was a young rookie. Josy froze. 'An apartment would be a dream come true!' But his conscience resisted. 'If I take this bribe, I will be compromising my values.' The next day, he filed his copy and the story was published.

In 2001, Josy went to Kashmir and met Abdul Majid Dar, the chief commander of the militant group Hizb-ul-Mujahideen. People wondered why he had met a terrorist. Josy responded, 'Conversations can create solutions and bring positive change.' He broke story after story and also wrote a book about corruption and crony capitalism. He asserted that the promoter of Jet Airways had close ties to India's most-wanted terrorist – Dawood Ibrahim. The airline and its promoter Naresh Goyal sued Josy for a thousand crore rupees. The day he heard the news, Josy was stressed and ran a high fever. But over the years, stress has become his new normal, and fear, his friend.

Does it bother him that bringing down corporates might cause thousands of people to lose their jobs? Josy replies, 'I feel bad for people working in corrupt companies. But jobs come and go. Investigative journalists are like moral marshals of society. That's why it's a great profession.'

Decades later, Josy was once again offered the bribe of a house to suppress a story. He asked the public relations head of a billionaire at a meeting in Khan Market, 'What kind of a house? Like this one here?' He pointed to a fancy house nearby. The flustered man said, 'Yes, yes! I am sure my boss will approve.' Josy, of course, didn't want the bribe; he was simply having fun.

'Money makes a difference,' Josy admits, 'but it is only a sixth sense that helps you enjoy the other five senses.'

Since 2019, Josy and his research team at Confluence Media have been hard at work, digging deep into history and current affairs to tell stories that challenge the status quo with facts.

Illustrated by Kokila Bhattacharya

T.M. KRISHNA

A MUSICAL MISSION

Three-year-old Krishna sat beside his mother's music teacher, tapping a stick on the ground in time with her singing. He too would soon begin his lessons. Once, when Krishna and his mother were visiting friends during Navaratri, someone asked him to sing, and he agreed. When Krishna finished his recital, he was offered a bowl of delicious sundal. 'This is great,' the boy thought. 'Every time I sing, I'll get a treat.' So, whenever someone asked him, he would readily belt out a song.

When he was twelve, Krishna participated in the Spirit of Youth concert series organised by the Music Academy. They wanted young artistes to perform at concerts held at the Academy's prestigious stage in Madras. Krishna was one of the youngest musicians there. He sang for seventy-five minutes, while his mother played the tanpura. Afterwards, a man approached him and said, 'You sang very well, thank you.' He handed Krishna a hundred-rupee note. The boy was delighted. For several years after the incident, whenever he performed, Krishna insisted his mother accompany him on the tanpura, wearing the same sari she wore at his first concert.

When Krishna was a little older, he heard D.K. Pattammal perform. By the end of the show, there were tears streaming down his face. He realised that, although it was only sound, music could leave a deep mark on a person. The memory of that first true understanding has stayed with him.

By now, people had begun talking about the young man with an incredible voice. Barely out of his teens, Krishna was already a rising star in Carnatic music. But, over the years, as he sang more and more, Krishna began to question what he was doing. 'I can push the right buttons and with a mix of the adrenaline, music, tempo and performance, I can play to the gallery easily.' He felt that it was a kind of manipulation.

Krishna became restless. 'I need to learn more,' he thought. He began researching the ragas he sang and the history of Carnatic music. Soon, he was full of questions. Why are ragas a certain way? Why must every concert follow a set pattern of performance? Who made it so? If music was truly transcendental, surely it should be able to exist without such rules?

Krishna's first act of musical activism was to break away from the traditional structure of a concert. Typically, a varnam is used as a warm-up before the performer gets to the meaty part of the performance. 'Warm-ups should be done at home,' Krishna thought. 'The varnam is a complex piece of music and should be the main part of my concert.' And this is exactly what he did. Many felt that Krishna was destroying Carnatic music tradition.

At home, Krishna had always been taught to be curious and ask questions. Once, he read an editorial about how young Carnatic musicians now had offices and secretaries and were inaccessible. Annoyed, Krishna wrote to the paper, asking the writer to 'Go ride a bullock cart if you don't like change'. He wrote lucidly on music and then on issues that agitated him, and one day found himself writing his first book. Now, he's written three.

One season, Krishna decided he would not perform, and simply cycled from venue to venue, listening to various musicians. It set him thinking. Why were only the same sort of people attending these concerts? For the next few years, he sang exclusively in the free and non-ticketed morning slots, so more people could access his music. But he still felt he was not connecting with new audiences. Perhaps the event itself was the problem? He decided never to sing at Chennai's famed December music season again.

Krishna and a friend had an entirely new idea. 'We should start a democratic music festival in a village along the beach.' So they did, and hundreds of people attended. It opened up questions about art, culture, caste, identity and value. Every year, it grew bigger and more performers joined in. Krishna then moved it to the streets of North Chennai, a part of town where people believed thieves, drug peddlers and other 'nefarious' characters thrived. He wanted to question this false stereotyping, and so he learnt about the people and was blown away by the local rap music and the food.

Over the years, Krishna has collaborated with various artistes as acts of solidarity, whether it is to protest violations of human rights or the diminishing space for freedom of expression. When world renowned cellist Yo-Yo Ma was in India, he and Krishna broke into an impromptu medley where they riffed off each other.

His honest engagement with musicians, writers and artists outside what is considered the 'classical' – and his critique of such hierarchies – have led to mesmerising performances, such as his concerts with the transgender community of Jogappas. People react differently to Krishna's activism. Some traditionalists write to him saying, 'I have thrown away your CDs.' Others say, 'I don't like your politics, but I like your music.'

Krishna has long stopped caring about what people think of his opinions. He continues to ask questions that disturb the powerful and stir up the status quo.

Illustrated by Ayesha Broacha

ABHILASH TOMY

AROUND THE WORLD

Abhilash was mesmerised. His father, a naval officer, had taken the six-year-old to the naval club and shown him the imposing hulls and dinghies stacked there. 'Wow! I want to sail for the rest of my life,' Abhilash declared.

One day, during his school holidays, Abhilash decided to go to the secluded beach near his home. But the beach was cordoned off with a fence. Abhilash climbed the fence and found large sheets of thermocol lying on the sand. 'This should work,' he thought, and crafted a makeshift raft. He found a long stick and went out into the sea aloft his new raft. His mother saw a child bobbing along on the waves from the balcony of their house. When he came back, she asked, 'Was that you on the water?' 'Yes,' said Abhilash. His mother looked at him sternly and said, 'Okay, just be careful.' And that was that.

When he grew up, Abhilash went to the Indian Naval Academy. Before he left, his father said, 'You are walking in as a boy, but you will come out a man.' The academy was hard work. Sometimes Abhilash thought, 'What is the meaning of this? Why are they making us do this?' But when he graduated three years later, he understood. Each and every graduating officer was now a gentleman.

At the academy, Abhilash had read a magazine about sailing around the world. He thought, 'This is what I want to do. I want to have my own boat and sail across the world by the time I am forty.' He started saving all the money he earned. In 2009, Abhilash volunteered to assist Commander Dilip Donde on the first ever circumnavigation around the world as part of the Navy's Sagar Parikrama programme. Dilip travelled solo and made only four stops during the entire journey, to refill supplies. Abhilash met him at all four ports to assist him.

Everyone knew Abhilash was keen to do a trip of his own. One day, an officer called him and asked, 'Abhilash, do you want to undertake the Sagar Parikrama 2?' Instantly, Abhilash replied, 'Yes sir!' Experts from the navy trained him. Then he was given charge of the Mhadei, the boat used by Commander Donde and named after the goddess Mandovi.

This expedition was different from the first. It was to be a non-stop, unassisted voyage. Abhilash had to carry everything he needed for six months – food, water, electricals, a reverse-osmosis water filter, tools, medicines. If he stopped to pick up anything, he would be disqualified.

Abhilash set sail from Mumbai in November 2012. He had to navigate, fix his own machinery, manage the cold and the heat, prepare his meals – it was not easy. He had some access to the internet, so while sailing, he started a blog and shared some posts. People around the country would avidly read them. Things were going well until the last few weeks, when Abhilash's water tanks got contaminated. He had only fifteen litres of water to survive on. 'I will use only sea water for everything but drinking and cooking,' he decided. After 151 days, he reached Mumbai to a warm welcome by President Pranab Mukherjee and other naval officers. He was now the first Indian to have completed a solo, unassisted, non-stop circumnavigation of the world.

When Abhilash took part in the Golden Globe Race in 2018, he raced against eighteen sailors around the world on very small boats, with no GPS, no electronics – nothing. On day eighty-two, he encountered a terrible storm. The boat turned upside down, and when he came up with it, he was on top of the mast. He fell and couldn't move. He messaged the race organisers: 'Rolled. Dismasted. Severe back injury. Cannot get up.' He managed to send out a few more messages before a rescue team reached him four days later. Back home, the doctors told him his spine was fractured. He had been hobbling around for days with a broken spine! Abhilash underwent a surgery and metal rods were inserted in his back. Within a few weeks, he reported back to duty.

Now Abhilash does what he does best – sailing. Ten years after his first Golden Globe Race, he entered the 2022 race and put his heart and soul into winning it.

Abhilash says, 'The sea is the best teacher. It teaches courage, patience, how to spend time, and will arm you with life skills – how to repair and manage things.' When asked if one needs an engineering degree to sail boats and fix them, he replied, 'The sea doesn't ask for any paper certificate. You learn on the job.'

ABHILASH TOMY

Illustrated by Lamiya Chandorwala

RAHUL MISHRA

DESIGNER WITH DREAMS

Rahul was lying in his cool mud house in the village of Malhausi, curiously looking at the birds nesting on the roof. His mother grew all kinds of vegetables, including round, fat gourds that sat amidst the creepers climbing on to the roof.

In the village, school only started in the first grade, so Rahul was home-schooled until then. When he finally enrolled, his teacher said, 'Rahul is too bright for the first grade; let's move him to the second.' In five days, the teacher said, 'Let's move him to the third.' Within fifteen days of starting school, Rahul had moved three grades! He was only six.

Eventually, his father sent him to a boarding school in Lucknow. One day, he saw a calendar with an image of Krishna and his cows. 'I love these cows,' Rahul thought. He started drawing cows on his slate. While he continued to do well in studies, he became deeply interested in painting and sports. In the seventh grade, he decided he wanted to be an artist. 'How will I tell papa? He wants me to be an engineer or an IAS officer!' he thought.

Rahul went to Kanpur University to study science, but kept sketching in his free time. After college, he told his father that he wanted to study design and art. 'How can a man make a living from art?' his father said angrily. But Rahul was determined and applied to the National Institute of Design (NID) in Ahmedabad.

During his admission interview, a panellist asked Rahul if he had any questions. Rahul said, 'Will NID be able to challenge my father's notion that I cannot accomplish anything with this profession?' Rahul was accepted.

All his life, Rahul had excelled in both studies and art. He had walked into NID confidently, but within a week, his confidence was shattered. 'These people are incredible. Their technique, their style … I am nowhere near them.' So, Rahul took as many classes as he could and spent hours practising.

Then it was time for his first project. It was on textiles – each student was assigned one state and they had to design a collection for young people. Rahul was given Kerala. 'How will I do a project on Kerala? All they wear is a t-shirt and a lungi!' he lamented. He begged the lecturer to give him a different state, but the man refused. Rahul then travelled to Kerala and stayed with villagers. He saw their beautiful lightweight cottons and noticed small details in their craft and culture. He came back with a great project and was grateful that his professors had insisted he stick to Kerala while allowing him the freedom to explore.

While at NID, Rahul got a call to showcase his collection at the Gen Next platform at Fashion Week. The audience included stalwarts like Wendell Rodricks, Manish Malhotra and Sabyasachi, who gave him a standing ovation. Rahul thought, 'As a person, I was born in Malhausi. But as a designer, I was born in Kerala.'

Rahul went on to study at Istituto Marongoni in Milan. When he came back, he launched his own label. He was drawn to Indian handloom weaves and hand embroidery. He met embroidery artisans in Mumbai and was shocked to see how they lived – sharing small rooms in slums, away from their families, barely eating a vada-pav a day! Most of them were from the same village in West Bengal.

Rahul thought, 'Wouldn't it be nice if the craftsmen could live with their families?' He remembered his favourite professor at NID, M.P. Ranjan, quoting Gandhi: 'Any step you think about taking, think of how it can help the weakest person gain their own freedom – their swaraj.'

When Rahul was designing his new collection of hand embroidery for the International Woolmark Award, he convinced fifteen artisans to go back to their villages and work from there. 'What if we do not get enough work from you?' they asked. But Rahul won the award and had sufficient orders to keep his artisans busy. He could repatriate even more people back to their villages.

Later that year, he was invited by the Fédération de la Haute Couture et de la Mode to showcase his collection at Paris Fashion Week, alongside the legendary fashion houses of Dior, Valentino, Chanel, Louis Vuitton and Hermès.

Once, while walking the streets of Paris, Rahul saw his designs on mannequins at Colette. 'It's incredible that creations from a tiny village in India have reached the most important fashion window in Paris!' he thought happily.

Rahul now employs over three hundred artisans in the village of Baundpur. His brand values draw from Gandhi's vision of making villagers independent and successful. He believes in sustainability and dreams of someday employing one million village-based artisans and workers.

Illustrated by Priyanka Paul

DHRUV LAKRA

ALL THE RIGHT SIGNS

Dhruv was on his ninth-grade school trip. His parents had given him some emergency money. At a magazine stand, he surreptitiously bought an 'adult magazine'. But his teacher found out and confiscated it. When they reached his hometown, Jammu, his mother was summoned to school. 'Have you seen what rubbish he is reading?' Without batting an eyelid, she said, 'He is a teenager! What do you expect?' That's when Dhruv realised his parents were different. If things were ever blown out of proportion, they would support him – within reason.

A few years later, Dhruv left for Bombay. After finishing college, he joined a large financial firm, but wasn't quite happy. In 2004, a devastating tsunami hit the Indian coastline, killing countless people. Thousands of fisherfolk lost their livelihood. Dhruv heard of an organisation looking for people to work in the slums in South India and he signed up. They would go from village to village to help figure out how best to rehabilitate people.

During this time, Dhruv observed two things for the first time: extreme marginalisation of the Dalit community and opportunism by some NGOs. A better quality of rice was sent to the Brahmin communities, and lower quality rice to the Dalit villages. Dead bodies from the Brahmin communities were dumped in the Dalit villages. Such discrimination deeply affected Dhruv. 'How can the nation move forward if this continues?' he thought. He also came across some unscrupulous NGOs that were working in areas completely unrelated to rehabilitation but were scouting for opportunities to get a share of the tsunami funds.

An idea formed in Dhruv's mind. 'I want to create a business that has a social impact. But not an NGO – it needs to be a commercially viable, profitable company.' He applied for and secured a scholarship at Oxford. When he returned to Bombay, he began to experiment with ideas for his enterprise.

In Bombay, Dhruv travelled extensively by bus. Once, he started a conversation with a man sitting beside him. But the man didn't respond.

Dhruv realised he could not hear. That's when the idea came to him. He thought, 'Delivery boys do not need to speak, and the need for delivery services is high in India. Let me see if I can pilot a project with persons from the Deaf community.'

Dhruv started Mirakle Couriers in 2010, with a small team of three. From day one, he communicated with his team using Indian Sign Language (ISL). 'If I write and communicate with them, I will never learn ISL,' he thought.

Training was a challenge at first. Once, Dhruv was teaching an employee, Ganesh, to operate in an area he wasn't familiar with. He gave Ganesh a piece of paper with the delivery address on it. 'If you get lost, ask the local paanwala,' Dhruv signed. He then followed Ganesh discreetly. When Ganesh got lost, he went to the paanwala with the written address. The paanwala said, 'Go straight. It's the second building from the signal.' Ganesh stared blankly. The paanwala raised his voice and repeated the instruction but that, of course, didn't help. Dhruv didn't intervene, because he knew Ganesh needed to learn. But when he saw the paanwala get frustrated, Dhruv went to him and said, 'Sir, he is Deaf.' Perplexed, the paanwala said, 'So why can't he just tell me that?'

It was hard in the early days. People thought it would be tough to deal with those who couldn't hear or speak. Once, after delivering a package, a boy signed 'thank you'. The angry customer called Dhruv and said, 'Your delivery boy gave me a flying kiss!' Dhruv had to explain that his gesture meant 'thank you' in ISL.

Despite all the challenges, Dhruv kept at it. He employed Deaf women to handle the back-office logistics and Deaf men to do deliveries. Each person was assigned their own beat, so they could become familiar with the area. With WhatsApp, keeping in touch became easier.

Now, Mirakle Couriers employs 180 people, of whom fifty per cent are Deaf and all are underprivileged. They handle deliveries for one of the largest e-commerce companies in the country. 'These companies are not choosing us for charity,' says Dhruv. 'They have a strict delivery metrics that we manage just fine.'

In a country where companies struggle to integrate even a minuscule percentage of people with disabilities, Dhruv has created an entire profitable business. He says, 'People with disabilities must be made part of the mainstream and not isolated. Just as they integrate in society, the government and society must learn to integrate and function with them.'

Illustrated by Noopur Choksi

ABHINAV BINDRA

ACE MARSKMAN

Abhinav was at Doon school, reading a letter from his father. One line stood out: 'Try sport, son.' 'Sport?' thought the stout boy. 'I do everything to wriggle out of any physical training, and dad wants me to play a sport!'

Abhinav was always homesick at Doon, so after a year at boarding school, he went back to Chandigarh to be with his parents. There, his father introduced him to a new sport. Abhinav would line up cans and bottles in the garden and shoot them. One day, he asked their maid and her daughter to stand in front of him. 'Hold these balloons over your heads,' he said to them and confidently fired his air rifle. His mother was horrified. 'Abhinav!' she yelled. 'I will stop you from shooting if you ever use humans as targets again!' Abhinav did continue shooting – using beer bottles, then cough syrup bottles, and then medicine vials used for injections. As his targets got smaller, his love for shooting grew.

Abhinav's father soon got him a coach. Colonel Dhillon trained the boy, every day after school, using paper targets with ten concentric circles. He was to aim dead centre. One day, while shooting, he asked Colonel Dhillon for a glass of water. The colonel brought it to him, but Abhinav continued shooting. The colonel said, 'Abhinav, why did you ask me for water if you're not drinking it?' Abhinav quietly pulled out a paper target which he had hidden under the tablemat. He had shot only eight points and had been too embarrassed to let his coach see it.

When he was thirteen, Abhinav participated in the state shooting championships in Chandigarh and had a perfect score of 600/600, when the world record was 597/600. Sadly, the competition wasn't recognised by the International Sport Shooting Federation. At a shooting qualifier competition for the national championships, he again had a perfect score of 400/400. But the officials refused to believe it and accused him of using altered pellets. Even after they got written confirmation that the pellets were legal, the officials refused to change their stand. 'I'll show them one day,' thought Abhinav defiantly.

In the following years, Abhinav trained hard. At the Munich World Cup, he asked Heinz Reinkemeier, the sports psychologist and coach, 'Will you please be my trainer?' Reinkemeier agreed, and with his wife Gaby, took on Abhinav's training. Abhinav participated in numerous international competitions and went to train in America at the Olympic Center. 'The athletes here exude confidence,' he thought. 'In India, I am pulled down by the cynicism of the people in sports. No facilities – nothing.' He especially loved the big sign: 'It's not every four years, it's every day!'

At the Athens Olympics in 2004, two minutes before the competition, Abhinav couldn't find his pellets. Gaby rushed and got them in time, and Abhinav placed seventh. The press wrote scathingly about him. Then, at the World Cup in Zagreb, Abhinav won his first international gold!

During the 2008 Olympics, Abhinav was so wired that he couldn't sleep. He asked the team doctor for sleeping pills. But in true Indian style, she said, 'Go and meditate!' On the day of the competition, when Abhinav fired his sighting shot, he hit a four! 'What is wrong? Did someone tamper with my gun?' he thought. This close to the game, a gun was usually adjusted only by a couple of millimetres. But Abhinav had to adjust his by forty clicks. The contestant next to him thought, 'It's over for the Indian!'

But Abhinav was calm, shooting with ease and concentration. With each shot, he inched closer to the top of the leader-board. His family in Chandigarh was praying for him. His mother sent someone to the mithai shop but said, 'Do not buy the laddoos until I call you!' When Abhinav shot his last round, he wasn't sure of his score. He turned and Gaby gave him a thumbs up. 'Did I win?' he asked her when she hugged him. She said, 'Yes. Gold!' Meanwhile, in Chandigarh, the laddoos were brought and distributed. Abhinav Bindra had just won India's first individual Olympic gold medal. The media poured into his house, and Abhinav's mother had to send someone to buy sixty kilograms of laddoos!

After years of professional shooting, Abhinav finally retired in 2016. He now serves on the advisory committee of Go Sports, and is dedicated to developing young shooting talent in India.

PANKAJ ADVANI

ALWAYS ON CUE

Pankaj would watch his brother Shree and his friends playing at the snooker club near their home in Bangalore. One day he said, 'Shree, let me try too.' Shree handed him a cue. Ten-year-old Pankaj confidently leaned over the table and managed to pot the ball. He was hooked. Soon he was playing against his brother, his brother's friends, and senior players at the club. Much older players began partnering with him in 'doubles' matches.

Every summer vacation, Pankaj and his brother would go to Bombay to visit family. One summer, the Karnataka State Billiards Association held a camp. 'I can't be playing in a snooker club all my life. I need to aim for state-level games,' Pankaj thought. So, he and Shree applied to participate. The association only offered spots to players who were at least fourteen years old, but they saw how talented young Pankaj was, and made an exception.

Both brothers spent the first month of their vacation at the camp. Pankaj learnt all the standard shots in billiards and snooker. Afterwards, Shree went to Bombay, but Pankaj decided to use up his remaining holiday attending the second batch of the camp.

When Pankaj was eleven, he and Shree competed for the Sampath Memorial Cup against state and national level players. Both got a huge handicap, since they were not professionals. But to everyone's surprise, they reached the finals. Pankaj was not only young but also short, so the newspapers reported, 'Tiny Tot Pankaj Progresses'. Finally, Pankaj beat Shree and won the tournament. The president of the Karnataka State Billiards Association announced that Pankaj's playing fees would be waived for a year.

After his win, a journalist interviewed Pankaj. 'What do you want to do when you grow up?' he asked. Pankaj replied, 'I want to be a businessman.' Then, as an afterthought, he added, 'And I'd also like to become world champion one day.' Pankaj's picture was often in the newspapers, and his mother painstakingly pasted all the reportage in a scrapbook. She liked

Illustrated by Lamiya Chandorwala

that her sons kept themselves busy in a sport – unconventional though it was. It kept them focused and out of trouble.

Pankaj would often watch the games at the main tables, where only senior players were allowed to play. 'I really want to play there,' he thought. He approached Arvind Savur, the champion-player-turned-coach. 'Arvind uncle,' he said, 'will you coach me?' 'Sorry Pankaj,' Arvind replied. 'You are too short. I can't.' Disappointed, Pankaj started doing pull-ups and even tried basketball – anything to gain a couple of inches! – while continuing to play snooker. After a few months, Arvind approached him. 'I think you are ready, Pankaj. Why don't we start?' His dream was to make Pankaj a world champion. He never charged Pankaj a single paisa, and soon was like a father figure to him. Before long, Pankaj was participating in national and international competitions.

When he was sixteen, Pankaj went to Latvia for a tournament. While checking in, he was smitten by the tall, blonde woman at the reception – Olga. Every day, after his match, he would shyly go and hand her a small gift – a chocolate or a toffee. She would smile. But to his dismay, Olga soon began dating a tall, handsome Irish player – closer to her in both age and height than the young, lovestruck Pankaj.

At seventeen, Pankaj participated in a tournament in Jammu. He won the senior national title and became the youngest title holder in snooker. Later, he went to the World Snooker Championship in China. Although he lost a couple of matches in the preliminary stages, he went from strength to strength to finally take the trophy. It was his first world title, and he was also the youngest player from India to win. Since then, Pankaj has won twenty-five world championships over nineteen years, in both billiards and snooker. He is the youngest in the world to have done so and is also the most decorated sportsperson in the country.

Pankaj has an unorthodox style of playing. While the textbooks say that the cue must be parallel to the table, his cue swings up and down. Other senior players have made statements in the media, criticising his technique. Shree, now a sports mind coach, not only helped Pankaj deal with anxiety and performance pressure, but also counselled him on how to deal with criticism.

Over the years, Pankaj has learnt to respect the game and his opponents. Even if they criticise him, he simply says, 'I let my cue do the talking!'

A READING GUIDE

WHAT IS CASTE?

What if you were told that in your school, you had to do jobs that no one else in your class did, like cleaning the school bathrooms? Or that you couldn't take part in extra-curricular activities or enter certain areas? What if you were punished for no reason? What if no one at school shared their food with you? Or made fun of the food in your tiffin because it wasn't what they ate? What if you were not allowed to befriend or date certain people?

What if you were told that all of this was just because you were born into a 'low caste' family?

Millions of people in India are discriminated against every day. When people believe that they are better than others because they happen to be born into an 'upper caste' Brahmin, Kshatriya or Vaishya family, they believe in the caste system. The caste system in Hinduism originated centuries ago and is prevalent even today. It places power in certain people's hands and denies others their right to equality. Surprisingly, such discrimination has also crept into other religious communities in India.

Some people flaunt their caste by wearing markers like a sacred thread, coloured lines on their foreheads, or a certain type of clothing. They might believe that some people are untouchable and that doing manual or 'unclean' work is the job of other people. They might use separate glasses and plates for household staff, give staff their leftover food, or make them use a different kitchen or a service lift in the building. They might believe that they should only marry people of 'their own kind'. These are a few examples of how people keep the caste system alive, ensuring that society stays divided.

Dalits and some Adivasis are the worst victims of the caste system and many are considered untouchable by the 'upper castes', who make up less than twenty per cent of Indian society.

(With inputs from Malavika Binny and Namit Arora)

UNDERSTANDING MENTAL HEALTH ISSUES

A mental health illness is caused by a chemical imbalance or disturbance in some part of the brain. There are many types of mental illness. It can affect anyone – educated and uneducated, men and women, young and old, rich and poor. Some people are very happy for weeks and then suddenly they get very, very sad. Sometimes they can be disruptive and troublesome. This can last for weeks or months. The condition is called bipolar affective disorder.

Some people may be so sad (and for no obvious reason) that they may not be able to do anything for days. This is called depression. Depression can also manifest as an intense preoccupation with physical health. It is very common for depressed children to bunk school and be disinterested in studies because they are unable to concentrate.

Most mental health problems can be treated with medication and therapy. Only ten per cent of mental health patients require hospitalisation. Families, friends and classmates can play an important role in helping people with mental health disorders. You can start by accepting people the way they are, being patient, non-judgmental, and supportive of their needs. Don't shame people with mental health issues or be critical of their behaviour. Avoid using words like 'psycho', 'mad' or 'crazy'. And remember, mental illness is not the result of 'karma' or personal weaknesses. It's just like any other medical issue. You wouldn't make fun of a cancer patient, would you?

(*With inputs from Dr Kishore Kumar, The Banyan*)

UNDERSTANDING PERSONS WITH DISABILITIES (PWDS)

A disability is a condition which may restrict a person's physical, intellectual, psychiatric, sensory or mobility functions. They may be able to do certain things better, worse, or not at all. Every person's disability is unique to that person. Everyone is 'temporarily able bodied'. Disability can happen at birth, later, or due to old age. Injuries can also lead to a temporary disability.

Many people associate disability with wheelchairs and crutches, or with someone who is Deaf or Blind. Some believe PwDs should be in separate spaces for education and learning and even work. This is a form of discrimination.

It is important for all societies and governments to 'mainstream' PwDs. The world over, disability is looked at through the social lens; it exists because of barriers in attitudes, laws and policies that prevent the full inclusion of PwDs in society. We must offer equal rights to all and treat everyone as an equal.

We can integrate PwDs by making sure spaces are PwD friendly. This could include ramps, rails, larger bathrooms with support rails, tactile flooring, prominent signage, and other design elements.

People with a disability do not prefer the terms handicapped, special needs, differently abled, 'divyang' or uniquely abled. The UN has adopted the term PwDs. Using words like 'lame', 'blind', 'dumb', 'deaf' to insult others is something we should steer away from.

(*With inputs from Nipun Malhotra, Nipman Foundation*)

UNDERSTANDING THE CONCEPT OF LGBTQIA

(Lesbian, Gay, Bisexual, Transgender, Queer, Intersex and Asexual)

Some people believe that men should fall in love only with women and that women should love only men. But people are unique in how they love and are drawn to others.

A 'gay' person is attracted to others of their own gender. A transgender person is someone who does not identify with their birth gender. An intersex person is born with several variations of sex organs and chromosomes.

Language is broadening to become inclusive of people with different sexualities and preferences, and you can look these terms up further.

Same-sex marriage is allowed in over twenty countries, but not yet in India. India recognises a third gender. This includes members of the hijra community, as well as transgender and intersex persons.

None of these terms should be used as an insult.

(*With inputs from Danish Shaikh and Harish Iyer*)

WHAT IS PUBERTY?

When humans are a certain age, usually between ten and sixteen, the body undergoes certain changes to attain maturity. Girls become taller, their breasts and reproductive organs develop, they grow armpit, pubic and some facial hair.

As a girl matures, her body starts producing eggs inside the ovaries every month. When a sperm does not fertilise the egg in twenty-four hours, it dies. After fourteen days, the lining of the uterus sheds in the form of blood. This lasts between two and seven days and is called menstruation. It is also called a period.

Boys also mature, just differently. Their voice deepens and they begin to grow body and facial hair. The body also starts preparing for reproduction. The testicles enlarge, as does the penis. The testicles begin producing semen, which carries sperm, and comes out as a whitish fluid from the penis. This process is called ejaculation.

(*With inputs from Dr Sangeeta Saksena, Co-Founder, Enfold Trust*)

BIBLIOGRAPHY

1. A.P.J. ABDUL KALAM

Kalam, A.P.J. Abdul and Arun Tiwari. *Wings of Fire: An Autobiography of Abdul Kalam*. Hyderabad: Universities Press, 2018.

2. ABHINAV BINDRA

Bindra, Abhinav and Rohit Brijnath. *A Shot at History: My Obsessive Journey to Olympic Gold*. New Delhi: HarperCollins Publishers, 2014.

'Exclusive Interview with Abhinav Bindra'. NewsX (YouTube). https://www.youtube.com/watch?v=Mt-TB53aibk, accessed 2 September 2019.

'Walk the Talk'. NDTV (YouTube). https://www.youtube.com/watch?v=BlxqD-u5Lts, accessed 2 September 2019.

3. ANAND GROVER

Team Culture Lab. 'Anand Grover on the 5 Key Milestones in the Section 377 Battle'. Godrej India Culture Lab. https://indiaculturelab.org/blog/five-key-milestones-in-the-section-377-battle/, accessed 5 September 2019.

4. A.R. RAHMAN

Trilok, Krishna. *Notes of a Dream: The Authorized Biography of A.R. Rahman*. New Delhi: Penguin Random House, 2018.

Kabir, Nasreen Munni. *A.R. Rahman: The Spirit of Music*. New Delhi: Om Books International, 2011.

'Rendezvous with Simi Garewal A.R. Rehman Part 1 & 2.' Simi Garewal Official. (YouTube). https://www.youtube.com/watch?v=rdPi13FpvB0, accessed 23 August 2019.

'Fireside Chat with A.R. Rahman'. Talks at Google (YouTube). https://www.youtube.com/watch?v=2XXM6fc0zzw, accessed 23 August 2019.

5. ARVIND GUPTA

Gupta, Arvind. Books and Toys. http://arvindguptatoys.com, accessed 27 September 2019.

6. AZIM PREMJI

Dharker, Anil. 'Azim Premji: 'Being Rich Did Not Thrill Me'. *Open*. https://openthemagazine.com/columns/open-conversation/azim-premji-being-rich-did-not-thrill-me/, accessed 3 October 2019.

Jenkins, Anthony. 'Azim Premji: The Bare-bones Billionaire'. *The Globe and Mail*. https://www.theglobeandmail.com/report-on-business/careers/careers-leadership/azim-premji-the-bare-bones-billionaire/article4266406/, accessed 3 October 2019.

ET Bureau. 'With $21 Billion, Premji Azim Among World's Top Philanthropists'. *Economic Times*. https://economictimes.indiatimes.com/news/company/corporate-trends/azim-premji-raises-his-contribution-to-philanthropy-to-21-billion/articleshow/68393148.cms, accessed 3 October 2019.

'Leadership & Philanthropy: Kiran Mazumdar-Shaw in conversation with Azim Premji'. IIM Bangalore (YouTube). https://www.youtube.com/watch?v=Hg2ylkZh5qc, accessed 3 October 2019.

'Visionary Encounter Fireside Talk Series by Sudhir Sethi with Azmi Premji'. Chiratae Ventures (YouTube). https://www.youtube.com/watch?v=-yBoqVZLsOY, accessed 3 October 2019.

'A Chat with Azim Premji'. WIPRO Earthian (YouTube). https://www.youtube.com/watch?v=MV0F3lnSQfs, accessed 3 October 2019.

7. BHAICHUNG BHUTIA

Mohammad Amin-ul Islam, *Beyond the Goal: The Biography of Baichung Bhutia*. India: Penguin Random House India, 2014.

'From the Foothills to the Football Field I Baichung Bhutia I TEDxYouth@JPIS'. TEDx Talks (YouTube). https://www.youtube.com/watch?v=DGe0Hj5Cq2I, accessed 27 September 2019.

'On the tea trail with Baichung Bhutia in Darjeeling'. NDTV (YouTube). https://www.youtube.com/watch?v=s-Y-CokNG3k, accessed 27 September 2019.

'Baichung Bhutia's first TV interview after retirement'. NewsX (YouTube). https://www.youtube.com/watch?v=7TE7eJhQvlg, accessed 27

September 2019.
'Exclusive Interview: Baichung Bhutia on Indian Football on NOV 17, 2015'. Impact TV (YouTube). https://www.youtube.com/watch?v=gjDh5yL3K3E, accessed 27 September 2019.

8. DHRUV LAKRA

'Mystic interview: Dhruv Lakra'. Devika Mehta (YouTube). https://www.youtube.com/watch?v=D_VNuyUmt18, accessed 9 October 2019.

9. G. VENKATASWAMY

Mehta, Pavithra K. and Suchitra Shenoy. *Infinite Vision: How Aravind Became the World's Greatest Business Case for Compassion.* New Delhi: HarperCollins Publishers, 2018.
Ingrid Diep. 'How McDonald's Inspired the Success of an Extraordinary Eye Hospital'. *Insight Magazine.* https://www.insightnews.com.au/Article3/880/How-McDonalds-inspired-the-success-of-an-extraordinary-eye-hospital.
McKinsey & Company. 'Driving Down the Cost of High Quality Health care'. *Health International.* https://www.mckinsey.com/~/media/mckinsey/dotcom/client_service/Healthcare%20Systems%20and%20Services/Health%20International/Issue%2011%20new%20PDFs/HI11_18%20AravindEyeCareSys_noprint.ashx, accessed 12 August 2019.
Manikutty, Sankaran and Kavil Ramachandran. 'Aravind Eye Care System: Retaining the Legacy'. *Harvard Business Review.* https://hbr.org/product/aravind-eye-care-system-retaining-the-legacy/ISB090-PDF-ENG, accessed 12 August 2019.

10. E. SREEDHARAN

Ashokan, *M.S. Karmayogi: A Biography of E. Sreedharan.* New Delhi: Penguin Random House, 2015.
'E Sreedharan Interview'. (YouTube). https://www.youtube.com/watch?v=gpTjMVp8gPQ, accessed 27 September 2019.
'Walk the Talk with E Sreedharan'. NDTV (YouTube). https://www.youtube.com/watch?v=9agFBKJfOP8, accessed 27 September 2019.

11. HOMI BHABHA

Venkataraman, G. *Bhabha and His Magnificent Obsessions*. Hyderabad: Universities Press, 2018.

'Documentary on Homi. J. Bhabha. A TIFR production. (Part 1-2)'. Shweta Ambekar (YouTube). https://www.youtube.com/watch?v=4ljlkVZ_AQM, accessed 30 August 2019.

'Documentary on Homi. J. Bhabha. A TIFR production. (Part 2-2)'. Shweta Ambekar (YouTube). https://www.youtube.com/watch?v=_2Cb0AlyHeI, accessed 30 August 2019.

12. I.M. VIJAYAN

'An Interview with I M Vijayan ll gnoTalks 2018 ll Avishkar 2018'. Media House of MNNIT (YouTube). Accessed 9 September 2019. https://youtu.be/bB_nN4BdnRk.

Sen, Debayan. 'IM Vijayan at 50: Celebrating one of India's greatest'. *Sony ESPN*. Accessed 17 September 2019. https://www.espn.in/football/india/story/3834435/im-vijayan-at-50-celebrating-one-of-indias-greatest.

Vijayan, I.M. 'Deer-Footed Magician'. *Outlook*. Accessed 17 September 2019. https://www.outlookindia.com/magazine/story/deer-footed-magician/299447.

13. J.R.D. TATA

Kuber, Girish. *The Tatas: How a Family Built a Business and a Nation.* New Delhi: HarperCollins Publishers, 2019.

Lala, R.M. *Beyond the Last Blue Mountain: A Life of J.R.D. Tata.* New Delhi: Penguin Random House, 2017.

The Tata Saga: Inspiring Stories from a Timeless Institution. New Delhi: Penguin Random House, 2018.

14. M.F. HUSAIN

Adams, Tim. 'MF Husain: The Barefoot "Picasso" of Indian Art'. *The Guardian*. https://www.theguardian.com/artanddesign/2014/jun/01/mf-husain-barefoot-picasso-indian-art-civilization.

Pal, Ila. *Husain: Portrait of an Artist.* New Delhi: HarperCollins Publishers, 2017.

'One on One – MF Husain'. Al Jazeera English (YouTube). https://www.youtube.com/watch?v=wqxUjuVPd8A, accessed 23 September 2019.

15. MURLIKANT PETKAR

Sharma, Sanjay and Medini Sharma. *Courage Beyond Compare: How Ten Athletes Overcame Disability and Adversity to Emerge Champions.* New Delhi: Rupa Publications, 2014.

'Interview with Mr. Murlikant Petkar – India's first Paralympic gold medalist'. Sportsindi (YouTube). https://www.youtube.com/watch?v=Px1gDs2lL5I, accessed 21 August 2019.

16. NASEERUDDIN SHAH

Shah, Naseeruddin. *And Then One Day: A Memoir.* New Delhi: Penguin Random House, 2015.

'Naseeruddin Shah Interview in 2004 Part 1/3'. (YouTube). https://www.youtube.com/watch?v=jZLH__45hVM, accessed 21 August 2019.

'Naseeruddin Shah Interview in 2004 Part 2/3'. (YouTube). https://www.youtube.com/watch?v=RLB71IsAYak, accessed 21 August 2019.

'Naseeruddin Shah Interview in 2004 Part 3/3'. (YouTube). https://www.youtube.com/watch?v=9DcW_-q4hXo, accessed 21 August 2019.

'Acting Advice Part 1| Naseeruddin Shah'. Join Films (YouTube). https://www.youtube.com/watch?v=LcbUtnkKDxU, accessed 21 August 2019.

'Acting Advice Part 2 | Naseeruddin Shah'. Join Films (YouTube). https://www.youtube.com/watch?v=_qlVm9dDOMw, accessed 21 August 2019.

'Walk the Talk with Naseeruddin Shah (Part 1)'. NDTV (YouTube). https://www.youtube.com/watch?v=rsa4_MPB5RA, accessed 21 August 2019.

'Walk the Talk with Naseeruddin Shah (Part 2)'. NDTV (YouTube). https://www.youtube.com/watch?v=J1Ne1u0PiIl, accessed 21 August 2019.

17. PANKAJ ADVANI

'Interview with Pankaj Advani'. GSTV (YouTube). https://www.youtube.com/watch?v=y1EKykotYuo, accessed 9 October 2019.

'Pankaj Advani on The Talk with Preethi Shenoy (Season 1)'. To Talk with Preeti Shenoy (YouTube). https://www.youtube.com/watch?v=PkObQ7p53KE, accessed 9 October 2019.

18. PULLELA GOPICHAND

Sharma, Sanjay and Sachi S. Sharma. *Pullela Gopi Chand: The World Beneath His Feet.* New Delhi: Rupa Publications, 2011.

'From Player to Coach: Pullela Gopichand Tells His Story I Exclusive Interview'. CNBC-TV18 (YouTube). https://www.youtube.com/watch?v=R4k9z3hQJmc, accessed 3 October 2019.

'Walk the Talk with Pullela Gopichand'. NDTV (YouTube). https://www.youtube.com/watch?v=jkUkGDRmpss, accessed 3 October 2019.

'Pullela Gopichand talks about lessons for Corporates from Indian Sports II NILF 2018.' Nasscom Events (YouTube). https://www.youtube.com/watch?v=0TsuI5LG1Kk, accessed 3 October 2019.

19. RAJENDRA SINGH

'Late 20th Century Folk Tale 1'. Soumitradey (YouTube). https://www.youtube.com/watch?v=rkslXYl8Fic, accessed 12 August 2019.

'Manoj Tibrewal Aakash Interviewed Mr. Rajendra Singh Waterman for DD News's Ek Mulaqat'. Manoj Tibrewal (YouTube). https://www.youtube.com/watch?v=On2Xocoyk_Q, accessed 4 September 2019.

'A presentation of ideas from India´s Waterman Dr. Rajendra Singh'. Goethe-Institut Chennai (YouTube). https://www.youtube.com/watch?v=HvEIS2eEpwg, accessed 4 September 2019.

20. RUSKIN BOND

Bond, Ruskin. *Lone Fox Dancing: My Autobiography*. New Delhi: Speaking Tiger Publishing, 2017.

21. SAM MANEKSHAW

Hanadi, Falki, *Field Marshal Sam Manekshaw*. New Delhi: Prabhat Prakashan, 2008.

'A life lived such - Field Marshal Sam Manekshaw'. A. Sudhakaran (YouTube). Accessed 24 September 2019. https://www.youtube.com/watch?v=qRmPmm7QeIE.

'Wonderful Interview of Field Marshal Sam Manekshaw with Karan Thapar-1999'. Sandeep Kulshrestha (YouTube). https://www.youtube.com/watch?v=D2z2L2B4Rio, accessed 24 September 2019.

22. SONAM WANGCHUK

'Sonam Wangchuk - The Real Rancho'. AVAHAN IPH (YouTube). https://www.youtube.com/watch?v=8e81ik4q_04, accessed 25 August 2019.

'Sonam Wangchuk, Engineer and Education Reformist I Interview'. News18 Tech (YouTube). https://www.youtube.com/watch?v=Y_RJclEX5s0, accessed 25 August 2019.

'Inside the making of Ice Stupas with Sonam Wangchuk in Ladakh'. Factor Daily (YouTube). https://www.youtube.com/watch?v=-1s0K_MKAgI, accessed 25 August 2019.

23. SUNDERLAL BAHUGUNA

James, George Alfred. *Ecology Is Permanent Economy: The Activism and Environmental Philosophy of Sunderlal Bahuguna.* Albany: SUNY Press, 2013.

Bhate, Shishir. 'Bahuguna's Diary'. *The Indian Express*, 19 June 1995.

Alvares, Claude. 'The Gentle Crusader'. *The Illustrated Weekly of India*, 23 June 1985.

Bahuguna, Sunderlal. *Fire in the Heart, Firewood on the Back.* Saliyara, India: Parvatiya Navjeevan Mandal, 1997.

'In conversation, Sunderlal Bahuguna with George James'. India 2003. https://www.india-seminar.com/2004/533/533%20in%20coversation.htm.

24. VERGHESE KURIEN

Verghese Kurien, *I Too Had a Dream.* New Delhi: Lotus Collection, 2017. https://www.youtube.com/watch?v=lD-TYoopahc&feature=youtu.be, accessed, 15 August 2019.

25. VIKRAM SARABHAI

Shah, Amrita. *Vikram Sarabhai: A Life*. New Delhi: Penguin Random House India, 2007.

26. VIKRAM SETH

Sethi, Sunil. 'An Interview with Vikram Seth'. https://sunilsethireader.wordpress.com/2016/08/18/an-interview-with-vikram-seth/, accessed 25 September 2019.

Gupta, Jitender. 'It Took Me Long to Come to Terms with Myself. Those Were Painful Years'. *Outlook.*

https://www.outlookindia.com/magazine/story/it-took-me-long-to-come-to-terms-with-myself-those-were-painful-years/232671, accessed 25 September 2019.

John, Shobha. 'I Got Drunk to Write'. *The Times of India*. https://timesofindia.indiatimes.com/home/sunday-times/deep-focus/I-got-drunk-to-write/articleshow/10888180.cms, accessed 25 September 2019.

Bhatia, Ritu. 'Delhi High Court Chief Justice Leila Seth Reveals a Mother's Trial with a Leap of Faith'. *Daily Mail India*. https://www.dailymail.co.uk/indiahome/indianews/article-2149010/Delhi-High-Court-Chief-Justice-Leila-Seth-reveals-mothers-trial-leap-faith.html, accessed 25 September 2019.

Davidar, David. '"Obsession Kept Me Going": Writer Vikram Seth on 25 Years of *A Suitable Boy*'. *Hindusan Times*. https://www.hindustantimes.com/books/what-kept-me-going-was-obsession/story-y2rTlzLUZBUmIJX22CmxiP.html, accessed 25 September 2019.

'Vikram Seth Part 1 I The Pritish Nandy Show I Episode 6 I PNC'. Pritish Nandy Com (YouTube). https://youtu.be/WPye-uIhxDs, accessed 25 September 2019.

'Vikram Seth Part 2 I The Pritish Nandy Show I Episode 6 I PNC'. Pritish Nandy Com (YouTube). https://youtu.be/Fs2vJeMbJ3k, accessed 25 September 2019.

'Vikram Seth Part 3 I The Pritish Nandy Show I Episode 6 I PNC'. Pritish Nandy Com (YouTube). https://youtu.be/NI46cgR3CIE, accessed 25 September 2019.

'Vikram Seth Part 4 I The Pritish Nandy Show I Episode 6 I PNC'. Pritish Nandy Com (YouTube). https://youtu.be/34C4h_BMEVg, accessed 25 September 2019.

'Una's Lecture: A Conversation with Vikram Seth'. UC Berkeley Events (YouTube). https://youtu.be/xPcl_q3nFBw, accessed 25 September 2019.

Woodward, Richard B. 'Vikram Seth's Big Book'. *New York Times*. https://www.nytimes.com/1993/05/02/magazine/vikram-seth-s-big-book.html, accessed 28 September 2019.

Mayes, Ian. 'A Ghost at the Oscars'. *The Guardian*. https://www.theguardian.com/books/1999/mar/27/books.guardianreview, accessed 29 September 2019.

Talati-Parikh, Sitanshi. 'From China, With Love'. *Verve Magazine*. http://www.vervemagazine.in/travel-and-spaces/vikram-seth-from-china-with-love, accessed 29 September 2019.

Rocco, Fiammetta. 'How We Met: Vikram Seth and Giles Gordon'. *Independent*. https://www.independent.co.uk/arts-entertainment/how-we-met-vikram-seth-and-giles-gordon-1453217.html, accessed 29 September 2019.

27. VISHWANATHAN ANAND

'Scroll Conversations I Viswanathan Anand'. *Scroll.in* (YouTube). https://www.youtube.com/watch?v=9OJNqcd2Nqw, accessed 25 September 2019.

'On the Couch with Koel - On the Couch with Viswanathan Anand'. Headline Today (YouTube). https://www.youtube.com/watch?v=LzdP KmBRiz0, accessed 25 September 2019.

'Rendezvous with Simi Garewal Vishwanath Anand & Aruna'. Simi Garewal Official (YouTube). https://www.youtube.com/watch?v=Ta3H6V67F-E, accessed 25 September 2019.

THE ARTISTS

ADWAIT PAWAR

'I illustrate for a living to pay for cat food so that my cats will let me live with them. I draw things that inspire me, things that I find funny and things that clients ask for.'

mail@adwaitpawar.com

AKASH RAJAN

is a design student about to graduate. A keen admirer of reptiles and a travel enthusiast.

akash.rajan2309@gmail.com

ANISHA THAMPY

is an illustrator and designer who lives in the real but comes alive in the surreal. She hopes to be able to design, illustrate and even write children's books some day.

foranisha@gmail.com

APARAJITA NINAN

Visualiser. Mum-er.
Food-er. Gin-er.

aparajitaninan@gmail.com

APARAJITHA VAASUDEV

is an artist, illustrator and graphic designer. She lives in Bangalore and enjoys getting her hands messy, indulging in art and craft, from oil portraits, concept art for films, to polymer clay jewellery.

aparajitha.vaasudev@gmail.com

AYESHA BROACHA

is a mean but passionate critic of art, brutally frank, and always looking to push the boundaries.

ayeshabroachaart@gmail.com

DEBANGSHU MOULIK

is a multidisciplinary visual artist based in Pune. He likes telling stories through pictures and spends a lot of time daydreaming and making things.

moulikdebangshu@gmail.com

HANISHA TIRUMALASETTY

is a self-taught artist currently based in London. She loves to create surrealistic illustrations and also happens to be the biggest fan of wearing black clothing and not smiling.

hanishatiru@gmail.com

JOANNA MENDES

is a freelance illustrator, linocut printmaker and music-lover. When she isn't drawing, she's busy chasing her spirited three-year-old.

mendes.joan@gmail.com

KOKILA BHATTACHARYA

is an illustrator, social activist and accidental entrepreneur. She loves to sleep and dreams of anarchy and the revolution.

kokila.nirvana@gmail.com

LAMIYA CHANDORWALA

is a visualiser by profession but a unicorn by nature. Her passion lies in creating thought-provoking and quirky designs.

lamiya.s.c@gmail.com

MAHA SATISH

Maha paints paws and the wet nose, and sporting actions striking a pose, books and brushes are all she knows, but pretends she is good at poetry and prose!

Maha.satish@hotmail.com

NOOPUR CHOKSI

Visual storyteller exploring the tangible and intangible relationships within the inner and outer realms of the human condition. Also loves pizza.

noopur.2013@gmail.com

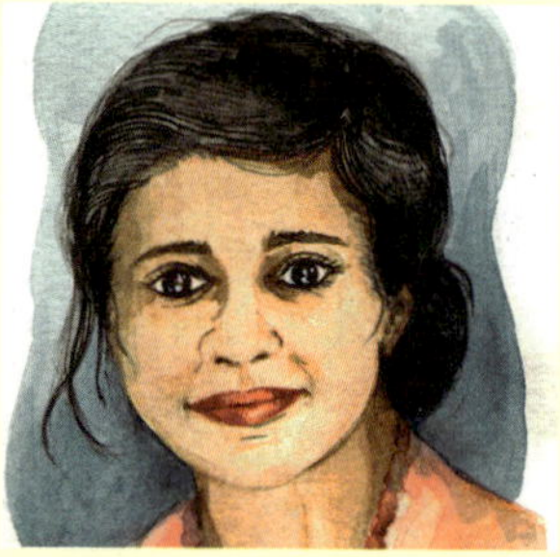

PRIYA KHATRI

is a communication designer obsessed with history, fact-finding, and storytelling - all of these find a unique place in her artwork.

khatri.priya@gmail.com

PRIYA KURIYAN

is a children's book illustrator and comics maker. She's happiest when filling her sketchbooks with strange caricatures of people in places she travels to.

priyakuriyan@gmail.com

PRIYANKA PAUL

is a twenty-one-year-old self-taught illustrator and poet. Her work revolves around the themes of social justice and self exploration. In her free time, she bashes trolls online and creates zines.

priyankapauly@gmail.com

RAE ZACHARIAH

is an Illustrator and animator. She gets her best ideas while listening to music and taking walks. She wishes she could produce her own music but is self-admittedly tone deaf.

raezack@gmail.com

SADHNA PRASAD

is inspired by everything bright and neon. She thrives in local spaces, food, markets, memories, colours and patterns.

sadhna.prasad1@gmail.com

SANCHITA JAIN
'A visual artist and communication designer based in India, I use illustration to channel my anxiety and give colour to my geeky sense of humour.'

sanchitajain17@gmail.com

SHANTANU SHARMA
is a designer and visual artist whose primary goal in life is to do great work and have fun doing it. He is currently slouched over his desk.

shantanu99sharma@gmail.com

SHIKANTH SABLANIA
aka 'Choorma' is a multifaceted artist working in the fields of visual art, graphic design, Illustration and comics.

shikhant.sablania@gmail.com

SHRUTI ANAND
Co-founder of Learn Something Different (LSD), a platform where creativity is nurtured. It is a space where all aspects of creativity come together to celebrate the diversity in articulation and expression. She is also a budding sculptor who likes creating funky ceramic masks and has a second-degree black belt in karate!

shrutianand1994@gmail.com

SUDEEPTI TUCKER
is an independent artist and illustrator with a base in New Delhi and Bangalore. Creating in both analog and digital mediums, her work explores ideas of femininity and expression while opening up dialogues about roots, identity and image.

sudeepti.tucker@gmail.com

SUJATA BANSAL
is a self-taught artist who loves sketching, reading, travelling and teaching art to children.

sujatabansal@yahoo.com

TANYA EDEN

'I live to travel the world, experience art and meet new artists around the globe. I also love adventure sports, diverse cuisines and pop culture.'

tanyaeden92@gmail.com

TARA ANAND

Is a Mumbai-based illustrator and artist making illustrative work centering on the lives of people around her.

taraanandillustration@gmail.com

UDISHA MADAN

'I have eventually started using my indecisiveness as a tool to play around and experiment with styles, mediums and forms, which is a great answer as to why it looks like I didn't make that.'

udisha.madan@gmail.com

ACKNOWLEDGEMENTS

One would think that after having written a similar book last year, this would be a cinch. But until the very last days before printing, I was wrapping up interviews with some of the men I write about here.

I have many people to thank.

At Westland, as always, my publisher V.K. Karthika, who had to constantly step in and send me encouraging messages to keep me going when I was exasperated and down. Her cheering from the sidelines and her skilful final edits have made this book what it is.

Vishwajyoti Ghosh and Sonakshi Singh for finding ways to lay the book out in interesting and captivating ways. Ateendriya Gupta, who did the first round of edits. Shrutika Mathur, who stepped in to work on the most annoying bit – the proofs. Vidhi Bhargava, who managed the entire process most patiently. Ajitha G.S., who offered deeper discussion and some valuable suggestions.

The efficient sales and marketing team, spearheaded by CEO Gautam Padmanabhan, who made *Like a Girl* such a success that I have the luxury to sit back, knowing that it will happen with this book too: Krishna Kumar Nair, Neha Khanna, Satish Sundaram and the entire sales force. And, of course, Vipin Vijay and the fantastic production team.

Ayesha Broacha, former classmate and art director, who was patient with every artist – guiding them, but leaving them room to interpret and develop the art to make it part of the book. To all the artists – some new, some who have worked with us before – thank you!

The men in this book who took the time to speak with me: Abhilash Tomy, Abhay Bang, Anand Grover, Arvind Gupta, Dhruv Lakra, Ganesh Devy, Josy Joseph, Pankaj Advani, Prashant Bhushan, P. Sainath, Rahul Mishra, Rajendra Singh, Romulus Whitaker, T.N. Seshan, Sanjeev Jain. To the relatives and friends of some of the men, with whom I was in touch for the stories: Vimla Bahuguna, Mukesh Khetarpal, Mallika Sarabhai and Arjun Petkar. Vikram, Shantum & Aradhana Seth

To the many people who helped with connects and inputs: Namrata Joshipura, Vandana Gopikumar, Janaki Lenin, Varun Menon, Aparna Ravichandran, Brigadier V.K. Nair, Krishna Trilok, Meenal Baghel, Michelle Pavri, Sandeep Unnithan, Gargi Rawat, Rasika Tyagi, Indu Lakra, Somak Ghoshal and Mahesh Rao. Rakhi Syaman, for taking time to translate an entire interview from Malayalam to English while in a cab, en route to work. Also, Nixon Fernando from Mr Seshan's office.

Nipun Malhotra, Dr Sangeeta Saksena, Malavika Binny, Dr Kishore Kumar, Namit Arora, Danish Sheikh and Harish Iyer, who provided expert inputs for the explainers at the back of the book.

Tejas Patel at Oxfam India, who fielded my persistent calls reassuringly.

My backbone – Peggy maami and Raja maamu (who also helped me with army contacts). My brother, Arjun. The kids – Aradhana, Arianna, Adianta, Adrish and Kaivalya. Family – Aditya, Abhinav, Nita and Joanna.

Dr Brijesh Siwach, who may have 'tortured' me with Bowen therapy but helped me stay mostly pain free for the writing of the book.

And my colleague Siddhant Trivedi, who painstakingly managed my life, the transcriptions, my appointments, and all the artists' deadlines.

If you enjoyed reading this book, do leave a review on amazon.in. Every review helps readers.

Please continue to follow the project on www.likeagirl.co.in on Instagram and send us pictures and stories of yourself (if you are a reader) or of children (if you are a parent or educator) reading the book. We would love to share them.

ABOUT THE AUTHOR

Aparna Jain is a leadership coach and an advocate for diversity and inclusion in the workplace.

She is the author of *Like A Girl: Real Stories for Tough Kids* (2018) *Own It: Leadership Lessons from Women Who Do (2016)*, which was awarded a Laadli Prize and was shortlisted for the Tata Literature Live Business Book Award 2016. She is also the author of *The Sood Family Cookbook* (2013).

Illustrated by Tara Anand